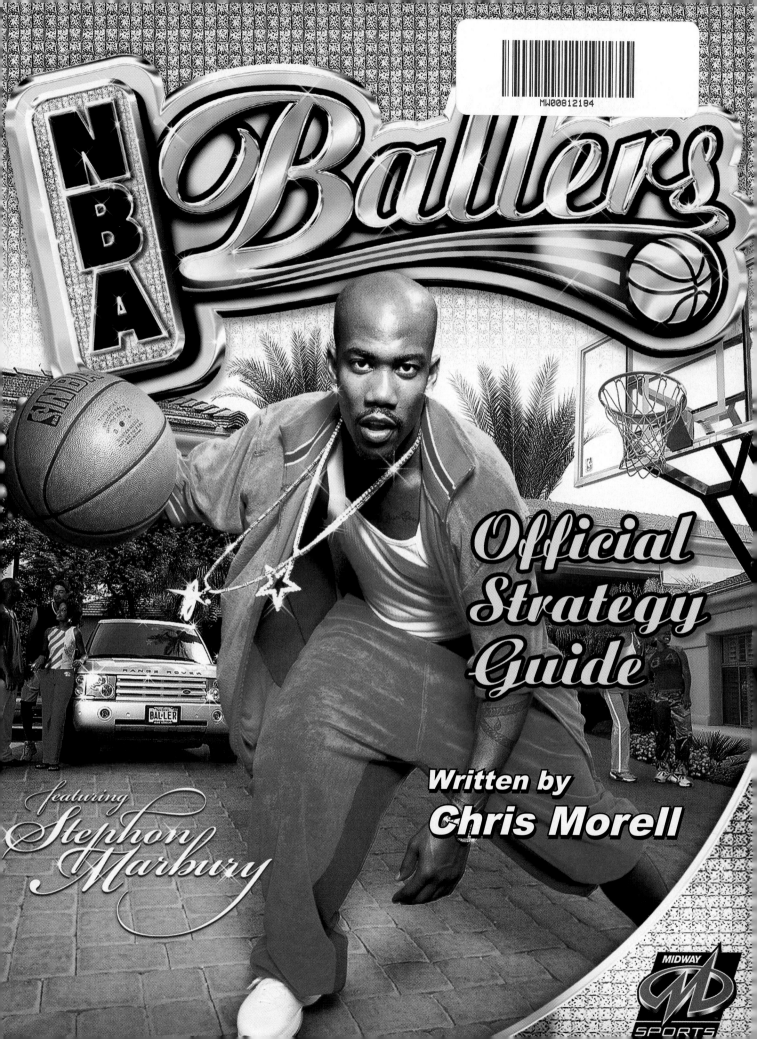

NBA Ballers

Official Strategy Guide

featuring **Stephon Marbury**

Written by
Chris Morell

MIDWAY SPORTS

DIMENSION PUBLISHING

Publisher	DAVID JON WINDING
Editor-in-Chief	GREG OFF
Senior Editor	MARK ANDROVICH
Associate Editor	CHRIS MORELL
Contributing Editors	ERIC WINDING
	ZACH MESTON
	THOMAS LAYTON
Design Director	STEVEN WANCZYK
National Advertising Director	MARK P. WINDING
CFO	SUSAN OLSEN-WINDING
COPY EDITOR	JEANNE HURST

|||||BRADYGAMES®
TAKE YOUR GAME FURTHER™

Publisher	DAVID WAYBRIGHT
Editor-In-Chief	H. LEIGH DAVIS
Creative Director	ROBIN LASEK
Marketing Manager	JANET ESHENOUR
Licensing Manager	MIKE DEGLER
Assistant Marketing Manager	SUSIE NIEMAN
Title Manager	TIM COX

The NBA and individual NBA member team identifications used on or in this product are trademarks, copyrighted designs and other forms of intellectual property of NBA Properties, Inc. and the respective NBA member teams and may not be used, in whole or in part, without the prior written consent of NBA Properties, Inc. ©2004 NBA Properties, Inc. All rights reserved. NBA team rosters are accurate as of February 8th, 2004.

ISBN:0-7440-0374-1
Library of Congress Catalog No.: 2004103738
Printing Code: The rightmost double-digit number is the year of the book's printing; the rightmost single-digit number is the number of the book's printing. For example, 04-1 shows that the first printing of the book occurred in 2004.
06 05 04   4 3 2 1
Manufactured in the United States of America.

Have you ever wanted to see your favorite NBA stars go head to head without eight other players on the court? Have you dreamed of seeing Magic vs. Bird, Kobe vs. LeBron, or Shaq vs. Yao? Welcome to NBA Ballers, the only street ball game where you can live out your one-on-one basketball dreams. Ballers is the first basketball game to incorporate a full-featured career mode. Rags to Riches lets you take a no-name baller, up from the streets, and pin him up against the NBA's best to become the most dominant player in the game. Then, take your player online and show off all your gear to your friends. So, pop in Ballers, boot up your console, and let's get started!

X-BOX

ACT A FOOL/STRONG STEAL

ALLEY-OOP/BLOCK-REBOUND

JUICE

JUICE

SHOOT/QUICK STEAL

MOVE PLAYER

PAUSE

JUICE

PASS TO CROWD/TAKE CHARGE

BACK 'EM DOWN

PLAYSTATION 2

ALLEY-OOP/BLOCK-REBOUND

ACT A FOOL/STRONG STEAL

BACK 'EM DOWN

SHOOT/QUICK STEAL

JUICE

MOVE PLAYER/TURBO

JUKE

PASS TO THE CROWD/TAKE CHARGE

PAUSE GAME

3

Player Bios

Player	Position	#	Height	Weight	D.O.B.	School
Shareef Abdur-Rahim	F	3	6-9	245	12/11/1976	California '99
Jason Terry	G	31	6-2	180	9/15/1977	Arizona'99
Allan Houston	G	20	6-6	200	4/20/1971	Tennessee '93
Allen Iverson	G	3	6-0	165	6/7/1975	Georgetown '96
Alonzo Mourning	C	33	6-10	261	2/8/1970	Georgetown '92
Antawn Jamison	F	33	6-9	225	6/12/1976	North Carolina '99
Antoine Walker	F	8	6-9	245	8/12/1976	Kentucky '98
Baron Davis	G	1	6-3	223	4/13/1979	UCLA '01
Ben Wallace	F-C	3	6-9	240	9/10/1974	Virginia Union '96
Chris Webber	F	4	6-10	245	3/1/1973	Michigan '95
Dajuan Wagner	G	2	6-2	200	2/4/1983	Memphis '05
Darius Miles	F-G	21	6-9	210	10/9/1981	East St. Louis HS (IL)
Dikembe Mutombo	C	55	7-2	265	6/25/1966	Georgetown '91
Dirk Nowitzki	C-F	41	7-0	245	6/19/1978	N/A
Eddie Jones	G	6	6-6	200	10/20/1971	Temple '94
Elton Brand	F	42	6-8	265	3/11/1979	Duke '01
Gary Payton	G	20	6-4	180	7/23/1968	Oregon State '90
Grant Hill	F	33	6-8	225	10/5/1972	Duke '94
Jalen Rose	F-G	5	6-8	217	1/30/1973	Michigan '95
Jason Williams	G	2	6-1	190	11/18/1975	Florida '98
Carmelo Anthony	F	15	6-8	220	5/29/1984	Syracuse '06
Jermaine O'Neal	F-C	7	6-11	242	10/13/1978	Eau Claire HS (SC)
Jerry Stackhouse	G-F	42	6-6	218	11/5/1974	North Carolina '97
John Stockton	PG	12	6-1	175	3/26/1962	Gonzaga
Karl Malone	F	11	6-9	256	7/24/1963	Louisiana Tech '86
Keith Van Horn	F	2	6-10	240	10/23/1975	Utah '97
Jamal Mashburn	F	24	6-8	247	11/29/1972	Kentucky '94
Jason Kidd	G	5	6-4	212	3/23/1973	California '96
Kenyon Martin	F	6	6-9	234	12/30/1977	Cincinnati '00
Kevin Garnett	F	21	6-11	240	5/19/1976	Farragut Academy HS (IL)
Kobe Bryant	G	8	6-6	220	8/23/1978	Lower Merion (PA)
Lamar Odom	F	7	6-10	225	11/6/1979	Rhode Island '01
Latrell Sprewell	F-G	8	6-5	195	9/8/1970	Alabama '92
Michael Finley	G-F	4	6-7	225	3/6/1973	Wisconsin '95
Tim Thomas	F	5	6-10	240	2/26/1977	Villanova '97
Mike Bibby	G	10	6-1	190	5/16/1978	Arizona '00
Darko Milicic	F-C	31	7-0	245	6/20/1985	N/A
Pau Gasol	F	16	7-0	240	7/6/1980	N/A

Player	Position	#	Height	Weight	D.O.B.	School
Paul Pierce	F-G	34	6-6	230	10/13/1977	Kansas '99
Predrag Stojakovic	F	16	6-10	229	6/9/1977	N/A
Rashard Lewis	F	7	6-10	215	8/8/1979	Alief Elsik HS (TX)
Rasheed Wallace	F-C	30	6-11	230	9/17/1974	North Carolina '97
Ray Allen	G	34	6-5	205	7/20/1975	Connecticut '97
Reggie Miller	G	31	6-7	195	8/24/1965	UCLA '87
Richard Hamilton	G-F	32	6-7	193	2/14/1978	Connecticut '00
Shaquille O'Neal	C	34	7-1	340	3/6/1972	Louisiana State '93
Shawn Marion	F	31	6-7	215	5/7/1978	UNLV '00
Stephon Marbury	G	3	6-2	205	2/20/1977	Georgia Tech '96
Steve Francis	G	3	6-3	200	2/21/1977	Maryland '99
Tim Duncan	F-C	21	7-0	260	4/25/1976	Wake Forest '97
Tracy McGrady	G	1	6-8	210	5/24/1979	Mount Zion Christian Acad. HS
Vince Carter	G-F	15	6-6	225	1/26/1977	North Carolina '99
Wally Szczerbiak	G-F	10	6-7	235	3/5/1977	Miami (Ohio) '99
Yao Ming	C	11	7-6	310	9/12/1980	N/A
Larry Bird	F	33	6-9	220	12/7/1956	Indiana State
Magic Johnson	G	32	6-9	255	8/14/1959	Michigan State
Julius Erving	F	6	6-7	210	2/22/1950	Massachusetts
Wilt Chamberlain	C	13	7-1	275	8/21/1936	Kansas
Bill Russell	C	6	6-10	220	2/12/1934	San Francisco
Isiah Thomas	G	11	6-1	182	4/30/1961	Indiana
Dominique Wilkins	F	21	6-8	224	1/12/1960	Georgia
Bill Walton	C	32	6-11	235	11/5/1952	UCLA
James Worthy	F	42	6-9	225	2/27/1961	North Carolina
Darryl Dawkins	C	53	6-11	261	1/11/1957	Maynard Evans HS (FLA)
Moses Malone	C	2	6-10	260	3/23/1955	Petersburg HS(VA)
Walt Frazier	G	10	6-4	200	3/29/1945	Southern Illinois
Kareem Abdul-Jabbar	C	33	7-2	267	8/16/1947	UCLA
Kevin McHale	F	32	6-10	225	12/19/1957	Minnesota
Robert Parish	C	00	7-1	250	10/30/1953	Centenary (LA)
George Gervin	G-F	44	6-7	185	4/27/1952	Eastern Michigan
Rick Barry	F	24	6-7	220	3/28/1944	Miami (FLA)
Pete Maravich	G	7	6-5	200	6/22/1947	Louisiana State
Earl Monroe	G	15	6-3	190	12/21/1944	Winston-Salem (N.C.)
Clyde Drexler	G	22	6-7	222	6/22/1962	Houston
Oscar Robertson	G	4	6-5	220	11/24/1938	Cincinnati
Nate Archibald	G	7	6-1	160	9/2/1948	Texas El-Paso
Willis Reed	C	19	6-10	240	6/25/1942	Grambling State
Wes Unseld	C-F	41	6-7	245	3/14/1946	Louisville
Steve Nash	G	13	6-3	195	2/7/1974	Santa Clara '96
Nene	F-C	31	6-11	260	9/13/1982	N/A
Jason Richardson	G-F	23	6-6	225	1/20/1981	Michigan State '03
Amare Stoudemire	F	32	6-10	245	11/16/1982	Cypress Creek (Orlando, FL)
Scottie Pippen	F-G	33	6-8	228	9/25/1965	Central Arkansas '87
Tony Parker	G	9	6-2	180	5/17/1982	N/A
Emanuel Ginobili	G	20	6-6	210	7/28/1977	N/A
LeBron James	F	23	6-8	240	12/30/1984	St. Vincent-St Mary HS (OH)

Player ID #	Position	Overall	Power	Speed	Stamina	Ball Handling	2 pt Short Range	2 pt Medium Range	3 Point	Dunking	Offensive Rebound	Defensive Rebound	Blocking	Steals	Free Throws	Clutch	Lay-Up	Low Off	Low Def
ABDUR-RAHIM	Forward	62	75	50	84	42	87	63	14	70	82	82	69	30	84	80	80	80	80
TERRY	Guard	58	26	78	81	82	72	65	62	13	31	31	30	71	88	64	62	41	22
HOUSTON	Guard	66	39	57	84	57	83	86	85	20	48	48	45	40	95	77	55	59	55
IVERSON	Guard	71	23	95	93	92	60	80	70	5	34	34	25	95	85	90	85	55	21
MOURNING	Center	63	85	45	69	30	91	55	10	80	86	86	90	38	71	76	89	85	92
JAMISON	Forward	70	61	80	85	31	82	74	51	75	77	77	63	20	79	70	63	73	70
WALKER	Forward	65	74	75	58	47	68	72	69	52	78	78	65	34	75	78	68	78	70
DAVIS	Guard	66	70	90	81	85	72	74	57	82	32	32	34	85	76	85	90	55	40
B. WALLACE	Forward	55	95	60	80	25	83	30	2	80	93	93	92	47	44	78	65	77	85
WEBBER	Forward	65	90	75	84	70	84	62	5	90	85	85	82	60	77	80	85	87	81
WAGNER	Guard	55	37	85	93	75	63	58	50	18	35	35	29	70	80	68	75	43	39
MILES	Forward	51	40	77	53	43	73	40	1	82	69	69	72	31	60	59	55	77	65
MUTOMBO	Center	55	81	35	77	20	69	32	1	70	90	90	95	24	77	66	81	82	96
NOWITZKI	Forward	67	70	52	89	70	85	80	65	70	83	83	82	37	88	72	75	75	70
JONES	Guard	65	51	74	81	74	73	69	52	75	62	62	66	90	82	71	62	67	67
BRAND	Forward	62	88	61	86	24	90	63	1	80	90	90	90	39	69	75	60	85	82
PAYTON	Guard	69	39	90	89	90	81	71	58	10	48	48	23	90	79	87	72	70	41
HILL	Forward	67	50	82	53	82	87	74	10	75	77	77	77	71	82	82	67	72	75
ROSE	Forward	71	47	86	88	83	72	61	45	65	63	63	55	72	85	80	88	73	60
WILLIAMS	Guard	65	40	87	90	90	68	70	65	1	35	35	5	84	70	69	72	30	20
ANTHONY	Forward	59	73	78	73	70	60	50	40	68	65	65	64	65	84	62	70	52	55
J. O'NEAL	Forward	68	81	60	84	49	84	68	15	84	88	88	87	37	73	73	82	79	86
STACKHOUSE	Guard	73	61	81	84	81	73	78	50	80	60	60	59	55	88	73	82	70	60
STOCKTON	Guard	61	30	80	64	85	87	80	70	1	29	29	5	88	88	87	90	25	18
K. MALONE	Forward	66	90	60	83	65	82	61	12	80	80	80	75	53	78	83	75	88	82
VAN HORN	Forward	62	65	57	64	65	87	66	35	70	79	79	65	41	80	70	75	78	70
MASHBURN	Forward	72	75	55	90	50	77	69	43	81	72	72	70	49	85	78	72	75	65
KIDD	Guard	70	57	93	80	93	73	78	44	50	45	45	39	93	84	84	90	63	48
MARTIN	Forward	67	85	80	71	49	83	74	16	73	82	82	90	64	65	68	75	78	82
GARNETT	Forward	73	80	85	88	82	89	70	55	88	91	91	85	74	81	78	92	83	82
BRYANT	Guard	86	73	92	92	92	88	80	70	90	77	77	72	90	84	91	85	77	72
ODOM	Forward	65	78	63	72	74	74	59	38	65	75	75	60	47	78	62	66	75	75
SPREWELL	Forward	67	54	80	85	81	70	74	45	75	60	60	57	66	85	80	81	65	60
FINLEY	Guard	70	49	80	82	81	75	70	50	85	71	71	54	79	86	59	65	68	72
T. THOMAS	Forward	76	60	73	79	75	81	70	68	80	72	72	56	74	81	78	82	74	78
BIBBY	Guard	68	32	90	75	91	83	76	75	1	32	32	22	77	85	85	80	34	17
MILICIC	Forward	49	43	50	61	24	57	63	30	30	42	42	72	47	73	67	60	60	60
GASOL	Forward	59	51	60	77	41	90	54	20	75	83	83	75	31	73	65	50	72	70
PIERCE	Guard	74	56	83	84	82	78	81	70	83	79	79	60	68	90	85	62	75	70

		Overall	Power	Speed	Stamina	Ball Handling	2 pt Short Range	2 pt Medium Range	3-Point	Dunking	Offensive Rebound	Defensive Rebound	Blocking	Steals	Free Throws	Clutch	Lay-Up	Low Off	Low Def
STOJAKOVIC	Forward	66	37	72	72	55	88	90	90	58	70	70	66	40	87	72	65	65	60
LEWIS	Forward	59	60	59	84	64	79	50	70	65	73	73	67	47	82	68	68	77	75
R. WALLACE	Forward	75	81	63	88	61	85	63	50	85	87	87	80	67	73	78	79	79	84
ALLEN	Guard	70	45	90	80	86	76	83	82	44	41	41	30	87	91	82	72	65	55
MILLER	Guard	64	25	68	54	70	75	84	86	25	44	44	48	64	92	95	52	63	55
HAMILTON	Guard	62	22	88	61	82	78	84	35	30	59	59	59	67	84	65	68	55	60
S. O'NEAL	Center	80	95	42	78	34	92	60	1	95	92	92	93	31	50	70	68	91	95
MARION	Forward	67	70	80	90	82	79	70	50	85	85	85	70	75	85	72	78	72	75
MARBURY	Guard	65	35	89	94	93	78	68	60	5	34	34	20	71	80	75	78	58	28
FRANCIS	Guard	66	27	90	90	90	78	62	52	80	31	31	25	85	80	90	72	35	29
DUNCAN	Forward	70	85	57	84	70	92	74	15	90	91	91	87	31	71	91	95	92	89
MCGRADY	Guard	80	55	90	88	82	87	80	53	92	76	76	72	76	80	89	78	78	70
CARTER	Guard	72	65	86	72	83	85	71	51	94	75	75	82	74	80	75	75	75	75
SZCZERBIAK	Guard	60	61	50	73	42	82	60	60	40	67	67	30	40	86	70	65	60	60
YAO	Center	57	82	45	79	20	90	48	2	83	81	81	92	20	81	60	80	83	80
BIRD	Forward	84	58	67	78	65	92	94	88	60	85	85	65	50	88	97	68	75	75
JOHNSON	Guard	85	70	68	77	95	92	84	70	60	81	81	66	50	85	97	73	77	70
ERVING	Forward	73	68	85	80	69	90	70	39	93	79	79	81	55	79	87	90	75	78
CHAMBERLAIN	Center	67	94	38	93	38	95	60	1	92	94	94	93	15	42	95	92	95	92
RUSSELL	Center	63	73	41	91	39	83	54	1	80	95	95	91	25	52	92	90	88	93
I. THOMAS	Guard	68	34	90	88	91	88	74	70	1	26	26	23	90	71	92	81	24	21
WILKINS	Forward	73	59	78	82	64	89	62	38	92	75	75	90	65	83	80	75	83	68
WALTON	Center	57	80	30	72	22	90	41	1	60	88	88	87	37	70	79	80	83	90
WORTHY	Forward	69	62	71	82	47	90	68	39	82	68	68	89	49	80	84	78	87	71
DAWKINS	Center	60	85	40	63	31	91	31	1	90	83	83	82	31	65	78	87	92	90
M. MALONE	Center	69	90	44	80	68	92	39	1	68	91	91	67	61	76	83	86	94	91
FRAZIER	Guard	65	30	81	85	85	92	58	30	10	30	30	21	80	75	80	68	63	24
ABDUL-JABBAR	Center	70	81	40	82	30	94	48	1	70	89	89	87	25	71	85	84	89	88
MCHALE	Forward	75	44	33	84	31	87	62	1	70	86	86	70	37	84	88	81	90	82
PARISH	Center	70	81	25	72	30	90	48	1	70	89	89	85	35	78	85	84	89	91
GERVIN	Guard	67	50	74	80	43	88	71	48	65	68	68	58	61	85	70	76	65	64
BARRY	Forward	66	39	61	88	68	87	80	50	10	41	41	31	92	87	90	76	60	64
MARAVICH	Guard	70	37	86	82	90	87	74	60	20	67	67	34	84	83	91	90	72	70
MONROE	Guard	62	40	74	75	74	80	81	46	1	48	48	22	77	83	75	58	55	27
DREXLER	Guard	71	47	80	76	82	86	67	65	87	76	76	74	84	81	85	81	78	75
ROBERTSON	Guard	75	34	84	91	92	87	79	40	40	75	75	34	81	85	92	85	75	60
ARCHIBALD	Guard	63	22	90	75	88	89	73	45	10	23	23	21	84	83	80	72	27	30
REED	Center	77	70	65	83	55	92	65	18	70	91	91	73	50	76	83	91	89	87
UNSELD	Center	75	70	60	70	52	91	68	12	65	92	92	66	60	64	82	83	87	87
NASH	Guard	66	27	88	67	84	83	74	71	1	28	28	20	84	92	83	52	58	23
NENE	Forward	53	89	42	50	27	88	50	1	80	75	75	80	37	57	63	78	60	76
RICHARDSON	Guard	69	70	81	68	81	70	69	67	87	67	67	76	68	77	70	75	59	64
STOUDEMIRE	Forward	67	71	82	58	49	81	79	15	85	83	83	87	31	66	67	72	81	73
PIPPEN	Guard	69	64	74	63	69	78	82	47	71	65	65	80	81	81	82	62	70	70
PARKER	Guard	65	30	87	71	82	80	59	64	14	30	30	23	77	75	78	65	21	18
GINOBILI	Guard	54	32	69	48	67	74	60	67	65	38	38	42	65	74	57	55	60	55
JAMES	Forward	80	73	78	70	85	70	80	60	90	60	60	70	80	85	80	90	70	72

Midway Ballers

Tips From the Experts

There are lots of different ways to play *NBA Ballers*. Some people are all about the flash, show-n-provin' with combos, taunts and stunt dunks, while others tend to be more conservative by keeping a close eye on their Juice meter and playing it slow. Below are a few examples of some playing styles that the b-ballers inside Midway Games use to play NBA Ballers.

THE TRE DAWG TRUE PLAYER STYLE

"My choice of players is an all around forward or big guard who has good dribbling skills and can hit the three. Play off me and I'll make you pay..."

FOULING

- The Tre Dawg True Player style calls for frequent fouling while on defense. It isn't just random hacking though, it is smart pushing -- Pushes close to the sidelines and on rebounds are a must when practicing this style.
- Always tries to keep fouls to four or lower until the final point of the round.
- Pushes when a player is going for a rebound to ensure he can get the board uncontested.

JUICE USE

- Uses Juice frequently, especially to get to the open spots for shots.
- Uses Juice when going for loose balls.
- Occasionally uses Juice to taunt and do attacking juke moves in an attempt to fill the house meter.

SPECIAL ABILITIES

- Uses special abilities only in certain situations.
- Uses back-in when he has an advantage.
- Uses alley Oops when a defender is playing him for the jumpshot.
- Uses pass to crowd to get open 3 Point shots or Hotspot shots.
- Prefers 2x Juice replenish, Back-In and Hotspots.

BRINGING DOWN THE HOUSE

- Rarely tries to win by Bringing Down The House, normally goes for the win on the score tip.

SCORING

- Uses pump fakes to get open shots.
- Uses Off The Hizzle and Pass To Self to stun opponent and get the open shot.
- Takes midrange J's whenever possible.

THE PITA POWER STYLE

"I like to play with a power forward or a center. My baller of choice has to not only hold it down in the paint, but also have the skills to hit that short range J whenever I need it."

FOULING

Uses fouls conservatively.

- Fouls only under the most optimal situations, such as jump shots or dunks.
- Tries not to send the opponent to the line during the first round.
- Rarely uses the Throwback move; normally pushes.

JUICE USE

Uses Juice in moderation.
- Never low enough so that he cannot execute a push if he needs to.
- Uses it occasionally on juke moves but is very aware of his defender's take charge tendencies.
- Uses Juice when he has an open lane which allows him to quickly get away from the D and give him an uncontested basket.

SPECIAL ABILITIES

Makes use of all special abilities
- Backs down in the paint but rarely finishes the button mashing battle. Pita tends to break out of the back-in and pull up for the J, giving him the open shot.
- Prefers special abilities 2x turbo replenish, Pass To The Sideline and Super Blocks.

BRINGING DOWN THE HOUSE

The house meter
- Pita tries to have his house meter at least half full by the end of the 1st round. This allows him to go down two different paths at the start of the 2nd round – Either win by bringing down the house or by beating out his opponent on the score tip. No matter the situation, Pita keeps the Bringing Down The House move in his back pocket.

SCORING

Scoring
- Always powers it inside.
- Always whips out the double clutch on contested dunks.
- Usually adds space between him and his opponent by tossing an Off The Hizzle or an Off The Glass pass so he can have the open J or drive to the lane.

THE JOHNNY BALLER FLASHY STYLE

"My Baller of choice is a well-rounded power forward. It is important that my Baller have decent dribbling skills, 'cause I like to dizzy my opponents with jukes, Act-A-Fool moves and Stunt Dunks, followed up with a slam. It is better to look good than feel good."

FOULING

Fouls *a lot* on defense
- Never fear fouling a player.
- Attempts to turn the ball over on every possession by pushing and shoving his way to the win – during jukes, dunks, shots, *anything!*
- HATES drawing the offensive charge, so he is very careful with attack jukes.

JUICE USE

Uses lots of juice
- Because Johnny Baller fouls so much, he uses a lot of juice. To compensate for this he only uses his Juice in short, limited spurts when running the court.
- Occasionally applies juice to his attack jukes, normally on the first move of a combo.

SPECIAL ABILITIES

Makes use of special abilities only in certain situations
- Stunt dunks are frequently used as combo finishers.
- Always uses the Pass 2 Sideline special ability, constantly passing out of rebounds and dunks to clear it quick and then call for the alley-oop. Also uses it to keep opponents off balance by passing, pushing and then calling for it back.
- Prefers special abilities Pass 2 Sideline, Super Blocks and Stunt Dunks.

Gameplay Tips

• Always use fouls wisely. You don't want to give up three-point opportunities for the free throw shooter. This swings momentum in the opponent's favor very quickly.

• When using pushes, use them near the sidelines whenever possible. This will make it easier to come up with the ball if he gets pushed out of bounds.

• Only attempt to pull a player back when he is between you and the basket. If you are between him and the basket and you attempt this maneuver, you can frequently give him an advantage to get to the basket and still be called for a foul.

• Challenge all shots taken by an opponent to lower his shot percentage.

• Use basic jump shots whenever possible. Leaners, quick shots, and fadeaways always have a lower percentage of success.

• On defense, use the strong steal as it has a higher chance of creating a turnover.

• When attempting a steal, always try to target the ball. This makes it easier to make contact and come up with the ball.

• On defense, attempt to take a charge when you need a change of possession. This move works well when trying to counter another player's offensive moves.

• Don't watch the ball when rebounding. Instead, watch the ball cursor on the ground to judge where the ball is going. If you're not sure when to jump, move your player toward the ball curser and use the auto rebound.

• Dive at loose balls whenever possible. Occasionally, you can come up with a loose ball even when your opponent seems to have beaten you to the ball.

• Use the Off the Hizzle whenever possible. This momentarily stuns your opponent and makes it easier for you to get an open lane to the hoop.

• When your player has the ability to pass to a friend, use it. It's like having a teammate on the court with you. If you have a three-point shooter and you want

BRINGING DOWN THE HOUSE

The house meter
• Always tries to have his house meter up at least three-quarters of the way at the end of the first round. This allows him to pull off a 5+ move combo at the start of the 2nd round and have his house meter totally full.

SCORING

Scoring
• Rarely attempts to score without putting the punk on his opponent first.
• Always tries to keep within one basket of the competition, even if it means turning the flash down for a possession.
• Likes working the baseline and scoring from underneath the basket.

---

to get open for a three, pass to your friend, fake to the basket, then go to the three-point line while calling for the pass back. This should get you an open three-point shot.

• When your opponent is playing loose defense, use your taunts. If your opponent is playing tight defense and you perform a taunt, it can knock him backwards and cause him to stumble. This should create enough time to complete your move. This helps increase your House Meter and gets you closer to Bringing Down the House on your opponent.

• Be careful when trying consecutive special moves against an opponent. He will normally be ready for the next move and shatter your ego. This results in a turnover and a loss of possession.

• When your opponent is playing tight defense, use the pass off the backboard. This will cause him to momentarily face the wrong direction just long enough for you to get by him. This also helps fill your House Meter.

• When using a large player with back-in ability, use it to your advantage. If your player has a better back-in ability than the defender, it will get you closer to the hoop for a higher percentage shot.

• When playing in Rags to Riches, play a balanced game. This ensures that you will have an all-around player as his attributes start to increase. If you only shoot threes or dunk, your player will become very one-sided and it will be difficult to compete.

• When playing in TV tournament, choose your player wisely. Always create a good match-up. Sometimes selecting small players will make it difficult to defeat a ladder of 7-foot players. Conversely, selecting a big guy to go against a ladder of speedy point guards can be a headache and require many retries. Choose wisely.

• If you execute one of the "taunt" moves while in close proximity to your opponent, it can knock him over. Always try to incorporate a taunt into a combo string to quickly build up your House meter.

• Some taunts cause the offensive player to place the ball on the ground and dance around it. If the defense attempts to steal the ball during these taunts, he will always miss it. You must dive on the ball to steal it during these taunt moves.

• You can perform the "Bringing Down The House" move from a crowd-assisted alley-oop. If you are having difficulty defeating a particular special rules match that requires you to bring down the house, try using this move instead. Dish it off to the sidelines, push your opponent, call for it back and bring it down!

• Defending under the hoop can be very difficult. Use this to your advantage! Drive the baseline often and toss up the shot or dunk the ball when you are directly under the hoop for maximum success.

THE VOLTIZZLE TURTLE STYLE

"I can choose any Baller I want and defeat you. It is all about timing and patience and my turtle style will defeat you."

FOULING

Rarely Fouls

- When it comes to fouling, the Turtle style plays more of a mental game than anything. Your opponent will either foul a lot more out of frustration that you aren't fouling or not foul at all, potentially removing a powerful weapon from their arsenal.

JUICE USE

Rarely uses Juice

- The Turtle style calls for very careful Juice consumption while on offense. Only when moving for an open shot, performing an attack juke or chasing after a loose ball should you use Juice. Do not use Juice while dribbling around the court.
- Since most defenders lay heavy on Juice and the Turtle style doesn't require any Juice usage while dribbling and moving around the court, your opponent will buzz around you attempting to steal the ball. This will force him to deplete his Juice and allow the Turtle to easily speed inside and take that uncontested J or dunk.

SPECIAL ABILITIES

Makes minimal use of special abilities

- The Turtle style requires one to play very tough defense and follow it up with a very simplistic offensive strategy to drive your opponent nuts.
- Prefers Hot Spots, Fire, and extra moves as the special abilities of choice.

BRINGING DOWN THE HOUSE

The house meter

- None. The Turtle style's simplistic offense does not make it a strong style if you like to Bring Down The House.

SCORING

Scoring

- Lots of outside shots. Shots from your player's Hotspot and right inside the three-point line are quite common when playing Turtle style.
- Rarely bring it inside except for the open lay-up or dunk.

- If you are getting blown out in the first round and you have managed to rack up four fouls, foul your opponent on his round winning basket. If he makes it he will win and won't be sent to the free-throw line, plus your fouls will be cleared for the next round!

- The Pass Off The Glass move is very lethal when playing with a mid-range shooter. This move cannot be countered if it makes contact with your opponent and really helps creates space for an open shot.

- If you have fouls to spare and you must score, dish the ball off to the sidelines and knock your opponent down with a push. He'll be on the ground and you'll be wide open for a pass back or an alley-oop!

- Even if you are wide open and driving the lane, it is always good to put a little extra space between you and your defender. With a trailing defender, throw an Off The Hizzle at him to gain just a little extra space and guarantee that score. He'll never see it coming.

- Some players jump high when dunking, giving you time to maneuver your player underneath them and set up to take a charge while on defense. Use this knowledge to your advantage and force turnovers and fouls.

- You can clear the ball by dishing it off to your friend on the sidelines. Try grabbing a board, dishing it off to the sidelines and calling for an alley-oop right away.

- On some of the harder difficulty levels, the computer can be a very tenacious opponent. The artificial intelligence in *NBA Ballers* tunes itself to your playing style, so change up yours approach by trying different strategies to help secure the win.

- Utilize both attack jukes and standard jukes when playing offense. The standard juke moves can be just as effective as the attacking ones, plus you'll never get called for a foul if you collide with your opponent.

Controls
Basic Offensive Moves

STANDARD JUMP SHOT
Press and hold the shoot button

COURT AWARENESS

This shot is the standard jumper. **INSIDE STUFF FROM MIDWAY:** While in the air, release the shoot button at your maximum height for the most accuracy. Releasing the button too early or too late will lower your shot percentage.

LEANER
Press and hold the directional pad or left analog stick toward the hoop and press the shoot button for a lean in jumper.

COURT AWARENESS

This shot is best used inside the three-point line, where its accuracy is much higher. Make sure to leave enough room between yourself and your opponent to avoid a blocked shot and a resulting shot clock violation. **INSIDE STUFF FROM MIDWAY:** The leaner is a good way to get a shot off if you need to shoot over your defender. Beware, though, that leanin' on the shot will lower your shot percentage.

FADE AWAY JUMPER

Press and hold the directional pad or left analog stick away from the hoop and press the shoot button to knock down a fade away jump shot.

COURT AWARENESS

Use a fade-away to arch a jumper over the outstretched arms of your opponent.

INSIDE STUFF FROM MIDWAY: The fade away shot is a difficult shot to block if the defender is playing tight defense. However, keep in mind that this off-balance shot is a lower percentage shot than a straight-up jumper.

HEAD FAKE

COURT AWARENESS

INSIDE STUFF FROM MIDWAY: If the defender is playing up on you tight, tap the shoot button to get your opponent in the air. Be careful though; once you pick up your dribble, you have to either shoot the ball or pass it off!

HOOK SHOT

Press the shoot button while running perpendicular to the hoop to pull off a hook shot, Kareem style!

COURT AWARENESS

INSIDE STUFF FROM MIDWAY: The hook shot is one of the most difficult shots to block, but it also comes with its own risks. The hook shot is a low percentage shot; the further you are away from the basket, the harsher the penalty.

DUNK/ LAY-UP

While running toward the hoop, press the shoot button to attempt a random dunk or lay-up

COURT AWARENESS

INSIDE STUFF FROM MIDWAY: Depending on the baller you choose, you will get a random dunk or lay-up based on the players tendencies in real life. Centers execute more dunks than lay-ups, whereas guards do more lay-ups than dunks.

DIVE

COURT AWARENESS

Make an attempt to dive for the loose ball on every blocked shot. INSIDE STUFF FROM MIDWAY: A dive can come in handy, but watch the ball carefully as it bounces. If you dive at the wrong time, the ball could bounce over you and leave the opponent with a chance to recover the rock and pop the easy shot.

FREE THROWS

When shooting a free throw, a meter will appear around a basketball on the bottom-left corner of the screen. When the clock counts down to zero, the meter will begin moving clockwise around the basketball, then back counter-clockwise around the ball. To shoot a perfect free throw, you will have to press the pass button directly in the middle of the red meter (power) on top, and then again when it reaches the blue meter (aim) at the bottom. The meter moves quick, and shooting free throws will definitely take some practice.

COURT AWARENESS

In NBA Ballers, free throws are even more important than in a five-on-five game. A made free throw awards a player with 3 points and possession.

THREE POINTS AND POSSESSION!

Basic Defensive Moves

QUICK STEAL

Press the quick steal button on defense to attempt a quick steal against your opponent. The quick steal doesn't require much commitment in position, so your opponent won't blow right past you.

COURT AWARENESS

INSIDE STUFF FROM MIDWAY: If you have a good defender, the quick steal can be a lethal weapon. However, guys with low steal ratings may have a hard time swiping the ball away when using this kind of steal.

STRONG STEAL

Press the strong steal button while on defense to perform a strong steal. This type of steal takes more body commitment than the quick steal, so you may be unable to stand your defensive ground.

COURT AWARENESS

The strong steal is useful against slower opponents. **INSIDE STUFF FROM MIDWAY:** If you are willing to take the commitment risk, the strong steal has a higher percentage of success. The strong steal is slower and takes longer to execute than the quick steal. Use the strong steal whenever possible to get that much-needed change of possession.

BLOCK

Press the block button on defense to block another player's shot. It is sometimes possible to catch your opponent's shot in mid air, rather than knock it away.

COURT AWARENESS

INSIDE STUFF FROM MIDWAY: If you hold down a juice button while blocking, you have a better chance to snatch the ball out of the air if your blocker has a high block rating. Hint: Always challenge a player's shot. Even if you know you're not close enough to swat the rock, if you attempt a block before he releases his shot you can greatly reduce his shot percentage.

TAKE CHARGE

Press and hold the take charge button to stand your ground and take the offensive foul.

INSIDE STUFF FROM MIDWAY: When positioned correctly, you can take a charge against a lay-up, dunk or attacking juke moves. Beware of the no charge zone under the basket, though; any charges taken in this zone won't count as a foul, and will knock your player on his backside!

DIVE

Press and hold the take charge button to stand your ground and take the offensive foul.

INSIDE STUFF FROM MIDWAY: When positioned correctly, you can take a charge against a lay-up, dunk or attacking juke moves. Beware of the no charge zone under the basket, though; any charges taken in this zone won't count as a foul, and will knock you player on his backside!

Advanced Offensive Moves

PLAYER SPECIFIC DUNKS & LAY-UPS

Any combination of the juice and shoot button (from inside the paint) will perform a dunk that is specific to each character.

DOUBLE CLUTCH SHOT

During a dunk, press the shoot button again to switch to a lay-up.

COURT AWARENESS

This is useful when you see that an opponent is about to block your shot. **INSIDE STUFF FROM MIDWAY:** The double clutch shot is useful if you feel a dunk is going to get blocked. Keep in mind that the double clutch shot may get you out of a sticky situation, but it has a lower shot percentage!

QUICK LAY-UP

While in a lay-up, press the shoot button again before your player is airborne.

INSIDE STUFF FROM MIDWAY: This move is a great way to get off a quick lay-up without having to worry about elevating to the hoop. The quick lay-up has a lower shot percentage over regular lay-ups. Use this movie if you've got the defender creepin' up on you and time is running low.

ALLEY-OOP

Press the alley-oop button to throw the ball into the air. Then, run toward the hoop while the ball is in the air to slam it home. Your player must have this special ability to pull off this move.

INSIDE STUFF FROM MIDWAY: If you want to throw off a defender, you can manually jump for the ball by pressing juice and the alley-oop button. Try it out if the defender is playing tight defense or if time is running out.

QUICK SHOT

Double tap the shoot button to get the shot off more quickly

INSIDE STUFF FROM MIDWAY: The quick shot is a great way to get a shot off if you think the defender is almost in range or time is running down on the clock. Your player won't jump as high and the chance that a quick shot is successful is lower.

PASS TO THE SIDELINE

While he has the ball, you can:

■ Move the right analog stick in any direction to perform a juke. This free ball juke is a great way to get around your opponent if he is trying to push you. Chances are he will miss!

■ Press the pass button and he will pass it back to you.

If you have a buddy on the sideline, you can press the pass button to pass him the ball. Your player must have this special ability to pull off this move.

If you wait too long to call for the ball back, your buddy will throw the ball away making it fair game for anyone!

■ Press the juice and act a fool button to try to grab your opponent and throw him out of the way. This makes it easier to get the pass back and not get your pass intercepted

■ Press the juice and the shoot button at the same time to try to knock down your opponent.

BACK 'EM DOWN

Press the back down button to get into position. Then, press the pass button repeatedly to overpower your opponent toward the basket. You can also use the right analog stick to spin out, or press shoot to take a shot from where you are. The following are your options while backing down an opponent:

- Quickly tap the pass button to move yourself and your opponent forward

- Move away from your opponent to spin out

- Press the alley-oop button to pump fake

- Press the shoot button to take a shot from where you are. Your player must have this special ability to pull off this move.

INSIDE STUFF FROM MIDWAY: Your player's low post offensive ratings determine how far your meter moves when you press the pass button. An opponent's low post defensive rating determines how far the meter moves back! More powerful players have a better chance of knocking down their opponents if they win the post up challenge.

PASS OFF THE BACKBOARD

Press any two juice buttons, then press the pass button to dish the ball off the glass.

COURT AWARENESS

The backboard pass is an easy way to build your house meter. **INSIDE STUFF FROM MIDWAY:** The backboard pass is a great way to create some space if the defender is playing tight defense. The further you are away from your opponent, the easier it is for him to block this pass. Make sure you are within close proximity when you try to put it on the glass.

ROBOTRON

Press and hold all juices and move the right analog stick to perform these fancy jukes.

INSIDE STUFF FROM MIDWAY: These moves can really show off some cool juke strings, but can leave you open to steals and pushes. Use this move to fake out those big blockers down low.

BRINGIN' DOWN THE HOUSE

INSIDE STUFF FROM MIDWAY: When the house meter is full, toss an alley-oop pass. While running to the basket, press and hold any two juice buttons before attempting a slam. When done correctly, you will see a haze around the screen. If the dunk is successful, you will tear down the basket and win the game!

To really show off, try calling for an alley-oop from your sideline buddy, then activate your house!

Any time you get a shot clock violation, you lose your entire house meter. Make sure you get the shot off!

PUT-BACK DUNK

Run under the basket and press the alley-oop button and the juice button to jam it back home. Your player must have this special ability to pull off this move.

COURT AWARENESS

Practice and perfect timing are the only ways to master this difficult put-back move. **INSIDE STUFF FROM MIDWAY:** If your player has this special ability run towards the rim and hold any juice button and press the alley-oop button to jam it back home.

TAUNT

Press and hold the left juice 2 button, then move the right analog stick in any direction to taunt your opponent. This increases your "house" meter and adds a trick to a pending combo.

COURT AWARENESS

INSIDE STUFF FROM MIDWAY: Taunts are a great way to sucker your opponent into a fifth foul, or to poke fun at his weak D. Although taunts will raise the house meter faster than any other move, they leave you open to steals and pushes.

ANKLE BREAKER

To execute an ankle breaker, simply move the right analog stick in whatever direction you wish to juke.

INSIDE STUFF FROM MIDWAY: If a defender is positioned correctly, he can take charge and draw a foul. You can trick your opponent by not holding down juice when moving the right analog stick. You won't break his ankles, but you can blow by your opponent without drawing a foul!

Act a Fool Moves

PLAYGROUND

Press the act a fool button to perform 1 of 30 different playground juke moves.

COURT AWARENESS

Playground moves are one of the easiest ways to build up and perform some intense combos.

OFF THE HIZZLE

Hold the right juice button 1 and press the act a fool button to throw the ball off your opponent's head, leaving him stunned.

OFF THE HIZZLE 2 OOP

Hold the right juice button #2, then press the act a fool button to throw the ball off your opponent's head and up for an alley-oop. Your player must have this ally-oop ability to perform this move

INSIDE STUFF FROM MIDWAY: You must be within the 3-point line to perform this move. Toss the rock off the opponent's noggin', then run around him.

STUNT DUNK

Press both right juice buttons while pressing the act a fool button to deal out some incredible moves. These are player specific stunt moves and dunks!

COURT AWARENESS

If you can pull 'em off, the Stunt Dunk moves are some of the flashiest in the game.

CLOWN'N 'EM

Hold the left juice button, then press the act a fool button while close to your opponent to clown him like a fool!

COURT AWARENESS

Clown'n 'Em moves are slow motion juke moves that will leave your opponent in your dust!

Advanced Defensive Moves

PUSH

Hold the juice button, then press the strong steal button to grab and push your opponent. Sometimes this will force a turnover, but it will always result in a foul.

COURT AWARENESS

INSIDE STUFF FROM MIDWAY: The push will always result in a foul. After 5 fouls, you opponent shoots a free throw so use them wisely.

WHILE BEING BACKED DOWN

When your opponent starts backing you down, you will notice a colored meter at the top of the screen. Repeatedly tap the take charge button to challenge him and push him away from the basket.

INSIDE STUFF FROM MIDWAY: Your low-post defensive rating determines how far the meter moves back.

SHATTERIN' THE EGO

Press the take charge button during the start of your opponent's Act a Fool move to interrupt it and steal the ball. This is called a combo breaker.

COURT AWARENESS

Pulling off a combo breaker requires pressing the take charge button at the perfect time, and can only be learned through practice. **INSIDE STUFF FROM MIDWAY:** You can counter Off The Hizzle, Off The Hizzle 2 Hoop, Stunt Dunks and Clown'n Em moves.

GAFFLIN' THE PASS

After your opponent passes to a friend in the crowd, try to intercept the ball on the inbound pass by standing in between the two characters.

COURT AWARENESS

When attempting to steal an inbound pass, make sure to give yourself enough time to get back and play defense if your opponent gets the ball back.

THROWBACK

Hold a juice button, then press the strong steal button to grab your opponent to the side. Sometimes this will force a turnover, but it will always result in a foul.

REBOUND
(LOOSE BALL ONLY)

If a ball is dancing on the rim, hold the Juice buttons and tap the block button to snag the ball off the iron.

INSIDE STUFF FROM MIDWAY: If you run under the ball without pressing a button, your player has a chance for an auto rebound if the ball is low enough. For better success at rebounding, move your player over the ball cursor, then jump at the appropriate time.

FREE THROW WAMMY

Press any button while your opponent is shooting a free throw to vibrate his controller and distract his shot.

Quick Play

If you are picking up the controller for the first time, you will want to spend a few minutes developing your skills in Quickplay mode before going head-to-head with the big dogs. You and your opponent's player are automatically chosen for you, so your player's specific moves and abilities will already be defined.

Games in NBA Ballers are played on a half-court, with two-point scoring up to eleven. You must win two out of three games to win a match, and a game is replayed if there is a tie when the clock runs out. Since you are not running a full-court game, you must clear a defensive rebound to the three-point line if the ball hits the rim. If your opponent doesn't draw iron, or you force a turnover, you can take it right to the hole (no clearance necessary). Develop your inside game first, then build your stats and work on the long-range shots and rebounds.

game rules
PLAY TO 11
WIN BY 2
BEST OF 3 ROUNDS
3 MINUTE ROUNDS
FIND HIDDEN MOVES

(1) PAYTON
Your Abilities
✓ Passing
Alley Oop
✓ Fire Mode
✓ Back In Mode
✓ Hot Spots
Put Back Dunks
Stunt Dunks
Super Blocks
Legal Goaltending
✓ 2x Juice Replenish
✓ Extra Moves
× continue

ROUND 1

KNOW THE RULES

While NBA Ballers is a street-ball type game, there are still standard rules and regulations to abide by, such as player fouls, a 15 second shot clock, and goaltending. Unless your player has a secret ability like "legal goaltending", you will have to choose your actions carefully.

Play Mode

This is where you will find the majority of NBA Ballers' gameplay. Unlike Quickplay, all the choices in the Play Modes menu allow you to choose your own player and/or opponent.

1 PRACTICE

Practice Mode allows you to tune-up your skills, without the consequences and restrictions of a normal game. Defense will be lax, and your opponent will not attempt to steal or block shots. This is where you can perfect Juice moves and combos, without a time limit, for use in tournament play.

2 1 VS. 1 VS. 1

This mode is a free-for-all, three-player game where each player is competing against each other. All setup screens and customization options are the same as in Versus Mode, with the only difference being the addition of an extra player. Since the court is a little more crowded, you may find it is sometimes tricky to perform routine moves and ball handling. The player with the lowest score gets possession after a basket, so try to stay on top.

3 VERSUS

After familiarizing yourself with some basic NBA Ballers gameplay, it's time to move on to the game's more advanced play. In Versus Mode, you can select your and your opponent's player from the game's list of available characters. You are given the option to choose from the standard or quickpick baller select style, the only difference being that the latter allows you to choose both players on the same screen. There are several player categories to choose from, and the only ones open to you from the get-go are standard Ballers East and West divisions. After confirming both players, the "select a crib" menu will appear. From here you have the option to change the game location, as well as adjust each player's handicap. You can also customize the game rules and enter codes before the match begins.

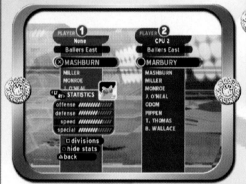

GAME MODE	DESRIPTION
No Custom Rules	Standard rules
Free for All	No ball checks or clearing
Do or Die	One round match
Break This!	The opponent's score is reduced by the value of the goal that you score. If you hit a 3, you take away 3 points from his score. Hitting a 2 pointer reduces his score by 2 points.
Goalie Match	Goaltending is allowed
Clearly Clean	No clearance necessary after a possession change
No Fouls	No penalization for fouls
Change Everything	Customize every rule

4 TV TOURNAMENT

The TV tournament progresses in episodes ranging from 4 to 8 matches each, with a designated purse of credits. Depending on the difficulty level, each episode will only allow you a certain number of continues. After completing an episode, you will unlock specific players for use in the rest of the game. There are a total of 19 episodes ranging from easy to hard in difficulty level, and from 100-300K in credits to win. This is where you will earn the bulk of your credits to acquire new cribs, rides, and gear. After selecting TV Tournament from the Play Modes menu, the episode selection screen will display everything you need to know about each tourney.

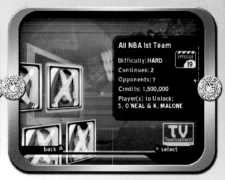

TV TOURNAMENT LADDER 1

RISING STARS

Opponent	Special Rules	3rd Player
Dajuan Wagner	-----	-----
Jason Richardson	-----	-----
Carmelo Anthony	-----	-----
Amare Stoudemire	-----	-----
Carmelo Anthony (unlock)	-----	-----

ROOKIE OF THE YEAR

Opponent	Special Rules	3rd Player
Vince Carter	MAKE IT, TAKE IT	-----
Allen Iverson	-----	-----
Chris Webber (unlock)	-----	-----
Steve Francis	FIRST 'JUICEHOUSE' WINS THE GAME, UNLIMITED TIME, UNLIMITED ROUNDS	
Jason Kidd	SHORTER SHOT CLOCK	-----

#1 PICKS

Opponent	Special Rules	3rd Player
Kenyon Martin		
Elton Brand	1 ROUND, UP TO 30 POINTS, NO FOULS	-----
Chris Webber	-----	Predrag Stojakovic
Yao Ming – NO CLEAR BALL	-----	-----
Lebron James	-----	-----
Kenyon Martin (unlock)	-----	-----

LAKER LEGENDS

Opponent	Special Rules	3rd Player
James Worthy	-----	-----
Kobe Bryant	HOLD YOUR OPPONENT UNDER 5 PTS	-----
Magic Johnson	MUST STEAL 5 TIMES AND WIN	Kareem Abdul-Jabbar
Wilt Chamberlain	-----	-----
Kareem Abdul-Jabbar (unlock)	-----	-----

CELTICS DYNASTY

Opponent	Special Rules	3rd Player
Nate Archibald	-----	-----
Paul Pierce	MAKE IT, TAKE IT	-----
Larry Bird	HOLD YOUR OPPONENT UNDER 8 PTS	-----
Bill Russell	-----	Robert Parish
Nate "Tiny" Archibald (unlock)	1 V. 1 V. 1	Paul Pierce (unlock)

DUNKFEST

Opponent	Special Rules	3rd Player
Vince Carter	-----	-----
Darryl Dawkins	GOALTENDING ALLOWED	-----
Dominique Wilkins	FOULS ARE OFF	-----
Julius Erving	IF YOU GO OVER FOUL LIMIT YOU LOSE THE MATCH	
Jerry Stackhouse	-----	-----
Dominique Wilkins (unlock)	-----	-----

3 POINT SHOOTOUT

Opponent	Special Rules	3rd Player
Jason Williams	-----	-----
John Stockton	WHILE ON FIRE, ALL SCORES PLUS 1, MINUS 1	-----
Wally Szczerbiak	-----	-----
Predrag Stojakovic	ONE ROUND MATCH	-----
Reggie Miller	-----	-----
Ray Allen	SHORTER SHOT CLOCK	Antoine Walker
Jason Williams (unlock)	-----	-----

RULES AND REGULATIONS

Opponent	Special Rules	3rd Player
Jason Terry	FIRST 'JUICEHOUSE' WINS THE GAME, UNLIMITED TIME, UNLIMITED ROUNDS	
Darius Miles	HOLD YOUR OPPONENT UNDER 5 PTS	-----
Latrell Sprewell	NO CLEAR BALL	-----
Kevin McHale	IF YOU GO OVER FOUL LIMIT YOU LOSE THE MATCH	
Jason Terry (unlock)	MAKE IT, TAKE IT	-----

UNITED NATIONS

Opponent	Special Rules	3rd Player
Emanuel Ginobili	-----	-----
Dikembe Mutombo	HOLD YOUR OPPONENT UNDER 5 PTS	-----
Predrag Stojakovic	-----	-----
Dirk Nowitzki	MUST STEAL 5 TIMES AND WIN	Steve Nash
Pau Gasol	1 ROUND, UP TO 30 POINTS, NO FOULS	-----
Emanuel Ginobili (unlock)	1 V. 1 V. 1	Darko Milicic (unlock)

OLD SCHOOL

Opponent	Special Rules	3rd Player
George Gervin	NO CLEAR BALL	-----
Wes Unseld	-----	-----
Clyde Drexler	HOLD YOUR OPPONENT UNDER 5 PTS	-----
Daryl Dawkins	-----	-----
Oscar Robertson	HOLD YOUR OPPONENT UNDER 8 PTS	-----
Dominique Wilkins	-----	Pete Maravich
Isiah Thomas	FOULS ARE OFF	-----
Clyde Drexler (unlock)	-----	-----

WILD, WILD, WEST

Opponent	Special Rules	3rd Player
Michael Finley	MAKE IT, TAKE IT	-----
Lamar Odom	-----	-----
Shawn Marion	IF YOU GO OVER FOUL LIMIT YOU LOSE THE MATCH	
Rashard Lewis	-----	-----
Antawn Jamison	FIRST 'JUICEHOUSE' WINS THE GAME, UNLIMITED TIME, UNLIMITED ROUNDS	
Rasheed Wallace	MUST STEAL 5 TIMES AND WIN	-----
Shawn Marion (unlock)	1 V. 1 V. 1	Michael Finley (unlock)

CONQUER THE EAST

Opponent	Special Rules	3rd Player
Richard Hamilton	SHORTER SHOT CLOCK	-----
Baron Davis	-----	Jamal Mashburn
Paul Pierce	HOLD YOUR OPPONENT UNDER 5 PTS	-----
Eddie Jones	FOULS ARE OFF	-----
Jalen Rose	FIRST 'JUICEHOUSE' WINS THE GAME, UNLIMITED TIME, UNLIMITED ROUNDS	
Baron Davis (unlock)	DO OR DIE	-----

KNICKS ALL STARS

Opponent	Special Rules	3rd Player
Willis Reed	SHORTER SHOT CLOCK	-----
Earl Monroe	-----	-----
Stephon Marbury	NO CLEAR BALL	-----
Walt Frazier –	NO RUFF HOUSING	Allan Houston
Willis Reed (nlock)	-1 V. 1 V. 1: HOLD OPPONENT TO NO 3'S	-----

PREP PRODIGIES

Opponent	Special Rules	3rd Player
Jermaine O'Neal	-----	-----
Lebron James	HOLD YOUR OPPONENT UNDER 5 PTS	-----
Moses Malone	MAKE IT, TAKE IT	-----
Kevin Garnett (unlock)	-----	-----
Kobe Bryant	IF YOU GO OVER FOUL LIMIT YOU LOSE THE MATCH	
Tracy McGrady	-----	-----

POINT GUARD CHALLENGE

Opponent	Special Rules	3rd Player
Steve Nash	1 ROUND, UP TO 30 POINTS, NO FOULS	-----
Stephon Marbury	-----	-----
John Stockton	SHORTER SHOT CLOCK	-----
Gary Payton	-----	Jason Kidd
Tony Parker	ONE ROUND MATCH	-----
Mike Bibby	HOLD YOUR OPPONENT UNDER 8 PTS	-----
Steve Francis (unlock)	-----	-----

TOWERS OF POWER

Opponent	Special Rules	3rd Player
Robert Parish		Bill Russell
Dikembe Mutombo	FIRST 'JUICEHOUSE' WINS THE GAME, UNLIMITED TIME, UNLIMITED ROUNDS	
Shaquille O'Neal	-----	-----
Bill Walton	MAKE IT, TAKE IT	-----
Wilt Chamberlain	-----	-----
Yao Ming	HOLD YOUR OPPONENT UNDER 8 PTS	-----
Bill Walton (unlock)	Fouled Out	-----

MVP'S

Opponent	Special Rules	3rd Player
Oscar Robertson		
Tim Duncan	FIRST 'JUICEHOUSE' WINS THE GAME, UNLIMITED TIME, UNLIMITED ROUNDS	
Allen Iverson	-----	Julius Erving
Bill Russell	ONE ROUND MATCH	-----
Wes Unseld	HOLD YOUR OPPONENT UNDER 8 PTS	-----
Larry Bird	1 ROUND, UP TO 30 POINTS, NO FOULS	Magic Johnson
Julius Erving (unlock)	-----	Allen Iverson (unlock)

ALL NBA DEFENSE

Opponent	Special Rules	3rd Player
Eddie Jones	WHILE ON FIRE, ALL SCORES PLUS 1, MINUS 1	-----
Ben Wallace	NO RUFF HOUSING	Kevin McHale
Alonzo Mourning	SHORTER SHOT CLOCK	-----
Karl Malone	-----	John Stockton
Dikembe Mutombo	MAKE IT, TAKE IT	-----
Kevin Garnett	FOULS ARE OFF	-----
Tim Duncan	-----	Gary Payton
Alonzo Mourning (unlock)	1 V. 1 V. 1	Dikembe Mutombo (unlock)

ALL NBA 1ST TEAM

Opponent	Special Rules	3rd Player
George Gervin	HOLD YOUR OPPONENT UNDER 5 PTS	
Kevin Garnett	FOULS ARE OFF	-----
Willis Reed	-----	-----
Jason Kidd	IF YOU GO OVER FOUL LIMIT YOU LOSE THE MATCH	
Kareem Abdul-Jabbar	-----	-----
Chris Webber	SHORTER SHOT CLOCK	
Shaquille O'Neal	GOALTENDING ALLOWED	Karl Malone
Moses Malone (unlock)	-1 V. 1 V. 1; FOULED OUT	George Gervin (unlock)

TV TOURNAMENT LADDER 2

RISING STARS

Opponent	Special Rules	3rd Player
Amare Stoudemire	-----	-----
Darko Milicic	-----	-----
Dajuan Wagner	1 ROUND, UP TO 30 POINTS, NO FOULS	-----
Carmelo Anthony (unlock)	-----	-----

ROOKIE OF THE YEAR

Opponent	Special Rules	3rd Player
Vince Carter	HOLD YOUR OPPONENT UNDER 8 PTS	-----
Jason Kidd	-----	-----
Allen Iverson	NO CLEAR BALL	-----
Steve Francis	-----	-----
Chris Webber	-MAKE IT, TAKE IT	

#1 PICKS

Opponent	Special Rules	3rd Player
Lebron James	HOLD YOUR OPPONENT UNDER 5 PTS	-----
Elton Brand	-----	-----
Chris Webber	No Ruff Housing	Predrag Stojakovic
Yao Ming	FIRST 'JUICEHOUSE' WINS THE GAME, UNLIMITED TIME, UNLIMITED ROUNDS	
Kenyon Martin	-----	-----

LAKER LEGENDS

Opponent	Special Rules	3rd Player
James Worthy	FOULS ARE OFF	-----
Kobe Bryant	HOLD YOUR OPPONENT UNDER 8 PTS	-----
Magic Johnson	-----	Wilt Chamberlain
Kareem Abdul-Jabbar	NO CLEAR BALL	-----

CELTICS DYNASTY

Opponent	Special Rules	3rd Player
Bill Russell	-----	-----
Larry Bird	SHORTER SHOT CLOCK	-----
Bill Walton	NO CLEAR BALL	-----
Paul Pierce	-----	Nate Archibald

DUNKFEST

Opponent	Special Rules	3rd Player
Grant Hill	MAKE IT, TAKE IT	-----
Darryl Dawkins	FOULS ARE OFF	-----
Jerry Stackhouse	-----	
Julius Erving	HOLD YOUR OPPONENT UNDER 8 PTS	-----
Dominique Wilkins	-----	-----

3 POINT SHOOTOUT

Opponent	Special Rules	3rd Player
Ray Allen	HOLD YOUR OPPONENT UNDER 5 PTS	-----
John Stockton	-----	-----
Wally Szcerbiak	ONE ROUND MATCH	-----
Predrag Stojakovic	-----	-----
Reggie Miller	-----	Antonie Walker
Jason Williams	IF YOU GO OVER FOUL LIMIT YOU LOSE THE MATCH	

RULES AND REGULATIONS

Opponent	Special Rules	3rd Player
Kevin McHale	HOLD YOUR OPPONENT UNDER 5 PTS	-----
Darius Miles	NO RUFF HOUSING	Carmelo Anthony
Latrell Sprewell	FIRST 'JUICEHOUSE' WINS THE GAME, UNLIMITED TIME, UNLIMITED ROUNDS	
Jason Terry	MAKE IT, TAKE IT	-----

UNITED NATIONS

Opponent	Special Rules	3rd Player
Pau Gason	FIRST 'JUICEHOUSE' WINS THE GAME, UNLIMITED TIME, UNLIMITED ROUNDS	
Nene	FOULS ARE OFF	-----
Tony Parker	-----	-----
Dirk Nowitzki	NO RUFF HOUSING	Steve Nash
Emanuel Ginobili	-----	Darko Milicic

OLD SCHOOL

Opponent	Special Rules	3rd Player
George Gervin	-----	-----
Wes Unseld	HOLD YOUR OPPONENT UNDER 8 PTS	-----
Isiah Thomas	-----	-----
Robert Parish	NO CLEAR BALL	-----
Oscar Robertson	-----	-----
Pete Maravich	-----	Rick Barry
Clyde Drexler	1 ROUND, UP TO 30 POINTS, NO FOULS	-----

WILD, WILD, WEST

Opponent	Special Rules	3rd Player
Antoine Walker	-----	-----
Lamar Odom	GOALTENDING ALLOWED	-----
Rasheed Wallace	-----	-----
Rashard Lewis	-----	-----
Antwan Jamison	HOLD YOUR OPPONENT UNDER 8 PTS	-----
Shawn Marion	-----	Michael Finley

CONQUER THE EAST

Opponent	Special Rules	3rd Player
Richard Hamilton	-----	-----
Jalen Rose	-----	-----
Jamal Mashburn	HOLD YOUR OPPONENT UNDER 5 PTS	-----
Eddie Jones	-----	-----
Baron Davis	SHORTER SHOT CLOCK	-----

KNICKS ALL STARS

Opponent	Special Rules	3rd Player
Allan Houston	NO CLEAR BALL	-----
Earl Monroe	MAKE IT, TAKE IT	-----
Walt Frazier	ONE ROUND MATCH	-----
Willis Reed	-----	-----

PREP PRODIGIES

Opponent	Special Rules	3rd Player
Jermaine O'Neal	-----	-----
Lebron James	HOLD YOUR OPPONENT UNDER 8 PTS	-----
Moses Malone	FOULS ARE OFF	-----
Tracy McGrady	-----	-----
Kobe Bryant	FIRST 'JUICEHOUSE' WINS THE GAME, UNLIMITED TIME, UNLIMITED ROUNDS	
Kevin Garnett	-----	-----

POINT GUARD CHALLENGE

Opponent	Special Rules	3rd Player
Nene	-----	-----
Stephon Marbury	SHORTER SHOT CLOCK	-----
Mike Bibby	HOLD YOUR OPPONENT UNDER 5 PTS	-----
Gary Payton	NO RUFF HOUSING	Jason Kidd
Nate Archibald	FOULS ARE OFF	-----
Steve Francis	-----	-----

TOWERS OF POWER

Opponent	Special Rules		3rd Player
Robert Parish	-----	-----	Bill Russell
Dikembe Mutombo	-----	-----	
Shaquille O'Neal	GOALTENDING ALLOWED	-----	
Yao Ming	MAKE IT, TAKE IT	-----	
Wilt Chamberlain	-----	-----	
Bill Walton	FIRST 'JUICEHOUSE' WINS THE GAME, UNLIMITED TIME, UNLIMITED ROUNDS		

MVP'S

Opponent	Special Rules	3rd Player
Oscar Robertson	HOLD YOUR OPPONENT UNDER 5 PTS	-----
Tim Duncan	1 ROUND, UP TO 30 POINTS, NO FOULS	-----
Larry Bird	-----	Magic Johnson
Karl Malone	NO CLEAR BALL	-----
Bill Russell	-----	-----
Julius Erving	-----	Allen Iverson

ALL NBA DEFENSE

Opponent	Special Rules	3rd Player
Ben Wallace	-----	-----
Ben Wallace	-----	Scottie Pippen
Latrell Sprewell	1 ROUND, UP TO 30 POINTS, NO FOULS	-----
John Stockton	-----	Karl Malone
Tim Duncan	HOLD YOUR OPPONENT UNDER 8 PTS	-----
Kevin Garnett	MAKE IT, TAKE IT	-----
Alonzo Mourning	-----	Dikembe Mutombo

ALL NBA 1ST TEAM

Opponent	Special Rules	3rd Player
Karl Malone	IF YOU GO OVER FOUL LIMIT YOU LOSE THE MATCH	-----
Kevin Garnett	ONE ROUND MATCH	-----
Willis Reed	-----	-----
Wes Unseld	FOULS ARE OFF	-----
Kareem Abdul-Jabbar	-----	-----
Shaquille O'Neal	-----	-----
Moses Malone	George Gervin	-----

RAGS TO RICHES

The network executives have done it again. Rags to Riches is a reality TV version of NBA Ballers where no-name street ballers are given the opportunity to live out every baller's dream: go head-to-head with real NBA stars. It's a long path ahead to achieve fame and fortune, but it will prove well worth the toil. If you make it to the top, you get to keep all the bling you've earned along the way.

After selecting a profile, you will come to the Custom Baller menu, a four step character creation process. On the first screen, you can customize your character's first and last name, birth date, position, number, move set, attitude, and nickname. Step two is the Define your Look menu, where you can alter all your physical attributes. Next, on the Develop your Skills screen, you must divvy out your skill points (400 to start) between 16 different player skills such as speed, power, and ball handling (you can also auto-distribute your points). Don't worry too much about where you put your skill points now; as you progress though the Rags to Riches story mode, you will be rewarded with many more.

After your baller is created and saved, you will be able to access the Nodify Baller screen every time you play in Rags to Riches mode. From here, you can change your gear, distribute skill points, and select your rides and friends. Make sure to check back frequently to see what you've earned.

Once you've gone the distance and completed the Rags to Riches story mode, your baller will be the most dominant player in the game! You will then be able to use him in other game modes and pin him up against your friends.

COURTSIDE TIPS

Some matches in Rags to Riches and TV Tournament modes have special gameplay rules you must follow to complete an episode.

■ **Hold Opponent Under 8 (H.O.U. 8)**
Play tight D in this mode, where the only way to win is to hold your opponent's score under 8 points.

■ **Hold Opponent Under 5 (H.O.U. 5)**
Some of the most difficult matches in the game occur with this special rule. Block shots, grab loose balls, and attempt as many steals as you can to keep your opponent under 5 points.

■ **Hold Opponent Under 3 (H.O.U. 3)**
Hold opponents under 3 points.

■ **No Fouls**
This special rule can work for or against you, as you and your opponent can commit as many fouls as you wish. Be quick on your feet to keep the ball in your possession.

■ **Fouled Out**
The user has five fouls to use in a round. If your player uses all five fouls, he automatically loses the match and "fouls out".

■ **Do or Die**
One round match (no "best of").

■ **Bring Down the House**
The first user to perform the "Bring Down the House" special wins the match. Unlimited time, unlimited rounds.

■ **Break This!**
The opponent's score is reduced by the value of the goal that you score. If you hit a 3, you take away 3 points from his score. Hitting a 2 pointer reduces his score by 2 points.

■ **Clearly Clean**
There's no need to clear the ball past the 3-point line in this special rules match. Grab a defensive rebound and put it back up for a quick score.

■ **House**
To To Bring Down the House, the player needs to do different jukes, crossovers, taunts, and defensive moves to fill up their house meter. Once the house meter is full you will hear the crowd chanting Juice House, Juice House. Once that occurs, move your player to the basket and press any two turbos and the triangle (alleyoop) button to bring down the house.

■ **Make It Take It**
In true street-ball style, you will be rewarded with possession for making shots. But, turn the ball over and you risk the chance of never getting it back!

■ **Steal the Ball 5 Times**
Grab, reach, push, and pickpocket your opponent at least 5 times.

■ **1st & 30 (no house)**
First player to score 30 points wins this one game match.

■ **Quick Clock (5 & 10 sec)**
In quick clock matches, you will have to get the ball in the air and out of your hands as quick as possible.

■ **No Roughhousing**
Fouling the player will get him possession of the ball.

RAGS TO RICHES LADDER

STREETBALL

Opponent	Special Rules
Ace	
Blaze	
Chaos	
Doc	
Frosty	
Ghost	

ALUMINUM TOUR 1

Opponent	Special Rules
Carmelo Anthony	
Darco Milicic	
LeBron James	1 ROUND, UP TO 30 POINTS, NO FOULS
Tony Parker	
Shawn Marion	
Amare Stoudemire	

ALUMINUM TOUR 2

Opponent	Special Rules
Willis Reed	FOULS ARE OFF
Earl Monroe	
Walt Frazier	

STAINLESS STEEL TOUR 1

Opponent	Special Rules
Dajuan Wagner	
Richard Hamilton	HOLD YOUR OPPONENT UNDER 8 PTS
Jamal Mashburn	
Rasheed Wallace	
Kevin Garnett	FOULS ARE OFF

STAINLESS STEEL TOUR 2

Opponent	Special Rules
Baron Davis	
Jason Williams	ONE ROUND MATCH
Allen Iverson	
Jason Terry	NO CLEAR BALL
Stephon Marbury	

STAINLESS STEEL TOUR 3

Opponent	Special Rules
Julius Erving	
Moses Malone	FOULS ARE OFF
Darryl Dawkins	

TITANIUM TOUR 1

Opponent	Special Rules
Grant Hill	NO CLEAR BALL
Jermaine O'Neal	
Gary Payton	
Eddie Jones	HOLD YOUR OPPONENT UNDER 3 PTS
Jason Kidd	

TITANIUM TOUR 2

Opponent	Special Rules
Darius Miles	
Jason Williams	FIRST 'JUICEHOUSE' WINS THE GAME, UNLIMITED TIME, UNLIMITED ROUNDS
Nene	
Scottie Pippen	MAKE IT, TAKE IT

TITANIUM TOUR 3

Opponent	Special Rules
Tim Thomas	
Tony Parker	HOLD YOUR OPPONENT UNDER 5 PTS
Shareef Abdur-Rahim	
Tracy McGrady	IF YOU GO OVER FOUL LIMIT YOU LOSE THE MATCH

TITANIUM TOUR 4

Opponent	Special Rules
Bill Walton	MAKE IT, TAKE IT
Isiah Thomas	1 ROUND, UP TO 30 POINTS, NO FOULS
Clyde Drexler	FIRST 'JUICEHOUSE' WINS THE GAME, UNLIMITED TIME, UNLIMITED ROUNDS

BRONZE TOUR 1

Opponent	Special Rules
Antoine Walker	HOLD YOUR OPPONENT UNDER 3 PTS
Predrag Stojakovic	
Ray Allen	
John Stockton	
Reggie Miller	HOLD YOUR OPPONENT UNDER 3 PTS

BRONZE TOUR 2

Opponent	Special Rules
Michael Finley	MAKE IT, TAKE IT
Allen Houston	
Mike Bibby	
Jason Kidd	MUST STEAL 5 TIMES AND WIN
Allen Iverson	

BRONZE TOUR 3

Opponent	Special Rules
Keith Van Horn	
Jerry Stackhouse	HOLD YOUR OPPONENT UNDER 8 PTS
Steve Nash	
Lamar Odom	
Steve Francis	HOLD YOUR OPPONENT UNDER 8 PTS

BRONZE TOUR 4

Opponent	Special Rules
Wally Szczerbiak	
Latrell Sprewell	FOULS ARE OFF
Ben Wallace	WHILE ON FIRE, ALL SCORES PLUS 1, MINUS 1
Chris Webber	
Karl Malone	

BRONZE TOUR 5

Opponent	Special Rules
Dominique Wilkins	HOLD YOUR OPPONENT UNDER 8 PTS
George Gervin	HOLD YOUR OPPONENT UNDER 5 PTS
Pete Maravich	

SILVER TOUR 1

Opponent	Special Rules
Guru	
Iceman	1 ROUND, UP TO 30 POINTS, NO FOULS
Jazz	
Legacy	
Lyric	MAKE IT, TAKE IT

SILVER TOUR 2

Opponent	Special Rules
Shawn Marion	SHORTER SHOT CLOCK
Jason Richardson	FIRST 'JUICEHOUSE' WINS THE GAME, UNLIMITED TIME, UNLIMITED ROUNDS
Tracy McGrady	
Kobe Bryant	WHILE ON FIRE, ALL SCORES PLUS 1, MINUS 1
Vince Carter	

SILVER TOUR 3

Opponent	Special Rules
Kenyon Martin	
Antawn Jamison	IF YOU GO OVER FOUL LIMIT YOU LOSE THE MATCH
Rashard Lewis	
Amare Stoudemire	NO CLEAR BALL
Shareef Abdur-Rahim	
Tim Duncan	

SILVER TOUR 4

Opponent	Special Rules
Wes Unseld	FOULS ARE OFF
Rick Barry	
Oscar Robertson	

GOLD TOUR 1

Opponent	Special Rules
Allen Iverson	ONE ROUND MATCH
Tracy McGrady	NO CLEAR BALL
Steve Francis	
Gary Payton	
Jason Kidd	SHORTER SHOT CLOCK
Kobe Bryant	MAKE IT, TAKE IT

GOLD TOUR 2

Opponent	Special Rules
Yao Ming	
Alonzo Mourning	HOLD YOUR OPPONENT UNDER 5 PTS
Ben Wallace	MUST HAVE MORE REBOUNDS THAN YOUR OPPONENT
Moses Malone	
Rasheed Wallace	
Dikembe Mutombo	
Shaquille O'Neal	GOALTENDING ALLOWED

GOLD TOUR 3

Opponent	Special Rules
James Worthy	
Kareem Abdul-Jabbar	
Wilt Chamberlain	
Magic Johnson	

PLATINUM TOUR 1

Opponent	Special Rules
Predrag Stojakovic	HOLD YOUR OPPONENT UNDER 5 PTS
Pau Gasol	
Steve Nash	
Emanuel Ginobili	1 ROUND, UP TO 30 POINTS, NO FOULS
Dirk Nowitzki	
Yao Ming	

PLATINUM TOUR 2

Opponent	Special Rules
Bill Russell	
Kevin McHale	
Nate Archibald	
Robert Parish	
Larry Bird	1 ROUND, UP TO 30 POINTS, NO FOULS

DIAMOND TOUR

Opponent	Special Rules
Jamal Mashburn + Baron Davis	
John Stockton + Karl Malone	
Richard Hamilton + Ben Wallace	NO CLEAR BALL
Kobe Bryant + Shaquille O'Neal	
Stephon Marbury + Kevin Garnett	
Steve Nash + Dirk Nowitzki	WHILE ON FIRE, ALL SCORES PLUS 1, MINUS 1
Steve Francis + Yao Ming	

SIGN A BALLER

Don't forget that there are other things to use your credit on besides a new pair of kicks. Use this feature to unlock specific NBA players along the way, for use in Tournament or Versus play. You can also access each player's stats by pulling up the statistics menu. Remember that any player not available in Sign a Baller mode must be unlocked either through TV Tournament or Rags to Riches mode. From this screen, you can also access the player stats menu.

Baller	Credits Required	Baller	Credits Required
Terry	460,000	Martin	840,000
Iverson	937,500	Garnett	1,175,000
Mourning	464,000	Finley	537,500
Davis	912,500	Milicic	492,500
Webber	727,500	Pierce	566,000
Mutombo	462,500	Marion	647,500
Williams	500,000	Francis	639,500
Anthony	675,000	Erving	1,300,000

Baller	Credits Required	Baller	Credits Required
Wilkins	950,000	Davis Alt. Gear	350,000
Walton	549,500	Webber Alt. Gear	350,000
M. Malone	875,000	Mutombo Alt. Gear	350,000
Abdul Jabbar	1,062,500	Williams Alt. Gear	350,000
Gervin	855,500	Anthony Alt. Gear	350,000
Drexler	985,000	Martin Alt. Gear	350,000
Archibald	655,000	Finley Alt. Gear	350,000
Reed	800,000	Milicic Alt. Gear	350,000
Ginobli	505,000	Erving Alt. Gear	350,000
Garnett Alt. Gear	350,000	Walton Alt. Gear	350,000
Francis Alt. Gear	350,000	M. Malone Alt. Gear	350,000
Wilkins Alt. Gear	350,000	Abdul Jabbar Alt. Gear	350,000
Iverson Alt. Gear	350,000	Gervin Alt. Gear	350,000
Mourning Alt. Gear	350,000	Drexler Alt. Gear	350,000
Pierce Alt. Gear	350,000	Archibald Alt. Gear	350,000
Marion Alt. Gear	350,000	Reed Alt. Gear	350,000
Terry Alt. Gear	350,000	Ginobili Alt. Gear	350,000

CUSTOM BALLERS

Just like in the Rags to Riches story mode, you will have the option to fancy up a new baller with everything he needs to show off his skills. It is the same exact customization process, except that this baller will be available for use in Versus and Tournament play.

The following is a list of all attire and accessories you can acquire credits and unlock with credit earned in NBA Ballers.

TOPS

T-SHIRTS

Baller	Credits Required to Unlock	Baller	Credits Required to Unlock
Razzle	Unlocked	Stop Sign	5,688
Napoleon Steve	Unlocked	Scout's Dream	5,744
Midway T	Unlocked	Slugfestivities	5,800
Jazzie Junk	3,500	Ramshackle	5,855
Mr. PT	3,500	Agent of Change	5,899
Chum	3,566	Hoo-chi Coo-chi	5,986
Indigizzle	4,000	Vocal Local	6,488
Da Blues	4,380	Source	6,500
Rainmaker	4,399	Make Your Mark	6,500
Green Light	4,500	Down From Uptown	6,533
Dub Deuce	4,577	Better Than Source	6,889
Wide Open	5,265	Where Brooklyn At?	7,500
Verzi Jerzi	5,500		

TANK TOPS

Baller	Credits Required to Unlock	Baller	Credits Required to Unlock
Black	Unlocked	Orange	5,345
White	Unlocked	Yellow	5,345
Red	5,345	Green Camo	5,876
Blue	5,345	Teal/Red Stripe	5,985
Green	5,345	Red/Blue Stripe	5,985
Aqua	5,345	Blue/Red Stripe	5,985

BOWLING SHIRTS

Baller	Credits Required to Unlock
JV's Light Hawaiian	Unlocked
Code 3	Unlocked
Jiggety Jazz	5,559
Supa Sonic	6,359
Ovens Emmissions	6,523
Hot Lava	6,535
Big Ballin Bowler	6,799
Dragon's Tail	6,855
Havana Heat	6,955
Jaded	6,955

GOLF SHIRT

Baller	Credits Required to Unlock	Baller	Credits Required to Unlock
Emerald	Unlocked	French Blue	6,299
MacMidway	5,099	Starmaker	6,533
Patriot	5,549	Alphonzo	7,599
Tommy D's	5,599	Runnin' Cool	7,599
Black & White	6,259	Mach 1.2	7,899

HOODIES

Baller	Credits Required to Unlock	Baller	Credits Required to Unlock
Bismarck	Unlocked	Dub O Trae's	7,000
Midway Madness	Unlocked	Flyin' Solo	7,241
Da Hood	5,799	Totally K	7,288
Stallion	6,455	NYC	7,500
Meistro	6,467	Glyphics	7,599
Lucky No. 7	6,500	Yeow 7s	7,599
High Five	6,599	Brooklyn	7,599
Pitaz	6,799	Mean Green	7,644
RGR 42	6,849		

JACKETS

Baller	Credits Required to Unlock	Baller	Credits Required to Unlock
Boulevard Blues	Unlocked	JB Maximus	8,566
Racer	8,159	Extra Ball	8,599
Twisted	8,233	RT Quitters	8,799
Jean Jacket	8,355	Brown Leather	8,999
Casual Like	8,355	KTR 2003	9,251
Skewlin'	8,488	Kiroa	9,255
Hello MrFancyPants	8,566	Black Leather	9,599

LONG SLEEVE SHIRTS

Baller	Credits Required to Unlock	Baller	Credits Required to Unlock
Midway Longsleeve	Unlocked	RU Ready	6,002
1 Numbah Onez	5,455	Dub Quintuples	6,233
Coderz	5,755	Agent Provocateur	6,455
Gear Down	5,988	MM 01	6,499
Mecha HI	6,000	Beat Ups	6,522
Urban 219	6,001	Area Codez 404	6,522

LONG SLEEVE SHIRTS (CONTINUED)

Baller	Credits Required to Unlock	Baller	Credits Required to Unlock
Country Clubbin'	6,533	Project NYC	6,976
Country Club	6,534	J Balla	7,599
Mmmmmmm	6,659	NY Metropolitics	7,855

NBA JERSEYS

Baller	Credits Required to Unlock	Baller	Credits Required to Unlock
Bobcats	8,500	Hornets	8,500
Bucks	8,500	Jazz	8,500
Bulls	8,500	Kings	8,500
Cavaliers	8,500	Knicks	8,500
Celtics	8,500	Lakers	8,500
Classic Bullets	15,599	Magic	8,500
Classic Celtics	15,599	Mavericks	8,500
Classic Hawks	15,599	Nets	8,500
Classic Jazz	15,599	Nuggets	8,500
Classic Knicks	15,599	Pacers	8,500
Classic Lakers	15,599	Pistons	8,500
Classic Pistons	15,599	Raptors	8,500
Classic Royals	15,599	Rockets	8,500
Classic Sixers	15,599	Sixers	8,500
Classic Spurs	15,599	Sonics	8,500
Classic Trail Blazers	15,599	Spurs	8,500
Classic Trail Blazers Alt	15,599	Suns	8,500
Classic Warriors	15,599	Timberwolves	8,500
Clippers	8,500	Trail Blazers	8,500
Grizzlies	8,500	Warriors	8,500
Hawks	8,500	Wizards	8,500
Heat	8,500		

NBA JERSEYS T-SHIRTS

Baller	Credits Required to Unlock	Baller	Credits Required to Unlock
Bobcats	8,500	Classic Jazz	15,599
Bucks	8,500	Classic Knicks	15,599
Bulls	8,500	Classic Lakers	15,599
Cavaliers	8,500	Classic Pistons	15,599
Celtics	8,500	Classic Royals	15,599
Classic Bullets	15,599	Classic Sixers	15,599
Classic Celtics	15,599	Classic Spurs	15,599
Classic Hawks	15,599	Classic Trail Blazers	15,599

NBA JERSEYS T-SHIRTS (CONTINUED)

Baller	Credits Required to Unlock	Baller	Credits Required to Unlock
Classic Trail Blazers Alt	15,599	Sixers	8,500
Classic Warriors	15,599	Sonics	8,500
Clippers	8,500	Spurs	8,500
Grizzlies	8,500	Suns	8,500
Hawks	8,500	Timberwolves	8,500
Heat	8,500	Trail Blazers	8,500
Hornets	8,500	Warriors	8,500
Jazz	8,500	Wizards	8,500
Kings	8,500		
Knicks	8,500		
Lakers	8,500		
Magic	8,500		
Mavericks	8,500		
Nets	8,500		
Nuggets	8,500		
Pacers	8,500		
Pistons	8,500		
Raptors	8,500		
Rockets	8,500		

NBA WARMUPS

Baller	Credits Required to Unlock	Baller	Credits Required to Unlock
Bobcats	8,500	Nets	8,500
Bucks	8,500	Nuggets	8,500
Bulls	8,500	Pacers	8,500
Cavaliers	8,500	Pistons	8,500
Celtics	8,500	Raptors	8,500
Clippers	8,500	Rockets	8,500
Grizzlies	8,500	Sixers	8,500
Hawks	8,500	Sonics	8,500
Heat	8,500	Spurs	8,500
Hornets	8,500	Suns	8,500
Jazz	8,500	Timberwolves	8,500
Kings	8,500	Trail Blazers	8,500
Knicks	8,500	Warriors	8,500
Lakers	8,500	Wizards	8,500
Magic	8,500		
Mavericks	8,500		

SUIT COATS

Baller	Credits Required to Unlock	Baller	Credits Required to Unlock
Flat	Unlocked	Jalapeno	11955
Figures	10500	Creamcicle	12499
Double Agent	10500	Keep It Clean	12500
Tantilizin'	10544	Icy Disposition	12999
Suit's Suit	10588	Doctor Is In	13000
Westside	11199	JBaller's Lustrous	13000
Grazin'	11487	Grafics	13000

CHAINS

SHORT

Baller	Credits Required to Unlock	Baller	Credits Required to Unlock
Silver Chain	Unlocked	Gold Links 2	7,599
Gold Links	7,500	Platinum Links	10,000
Gold Chain	7,500		

MEDIUM

Baller	Credits Required to Unlock	Baller	Credits Required to Unlock
Silver Chain	Unlocked	Gold Links	1,000
Gold Chain	1,000	Gold Links 2	1,000
Platinum Links	1,000		

LONG

Baller	Credits Required to Unlock	Baller	Credits Required to Unlock
Silver Chain	Unlocked	Gold Links	1,000
Gold Chain	1,000	Gold Links 2	1,000
Platinum Links	1,000		

MEDIUM MEDALLION

Baller	Credits Required to Unlock	Baller	Credits Required to Unlock
Silver Basketball	Unlocked	Crown	14,599
Silver Dawg	10,000	All Aces	14,855
Gold Basketball	10,500	Platinum 83	15,299
Gold 83	10,645	Star	15,899
Gold Dawg	10,799	Platinum Pendant	15,999
Gold Pendant	11,000	Platinum Baller	16,000
Gold Baller	12,000	Bling Basketball	17,000

LONG MEDALLION

Baller	Credits Required to Unlock	Baller	Credits Required to Unlock
Silver Basketball	Unlocked	Gold Baller	1000
Gold Basketball	1000	Crown	1000
Platinum 83	1000	Dragon	1000
Platinum Baller	1000	Bling Basketball	1000

WHISTLE

Baller	Credits Required to Unlock
Platinum Referee	Unlocked

TATTOOS

NBA JERSEYS

Baller	Credits Required to Unlock	Baller	Credits Required to Unlock
Iverson Sleeve	Unlocked	Rose Tattoos	10000
Kanji	5000	J O'Neal Tattoos	10000
Flames	5000	Hamilton Tattoos	10000
Sun	5000	Marbury Tattoo	10000
Panther	5000	Iverson Tattoo	10000
Barbwire/Flames	5000	Shaq Tattoo	10000
Bulldog/Celt1	5000	Garnett Tattoos	10000
Kanji/Tribal	5000	Francis Tattoo	10000
Panther/Celt2	5000	R Wallace Tattoos	10000
Panther2	5000	Stoudemire Tattoos	10000
Celt1	5000	Lewis Tattoos	10000
Bulldog	5000	Wagner Tattoos	10000
Tribal	5000	Terry Tattoos	10000
Celt1/Celt2	5000	Miles Tattoos	10000
Williams Tattoos	10000	Richardson Tattoos	10000
Mashburn Tattoos	10000	Martin Tattoos	10000
Anthony Tattoos	10000	McGrady Tattoos	10000
Thomas Tattoos	10000	Stackhouse Tattoos	10000
Bibby Tattoos	10000	Barbwire	Unlocked
Wallace Tattoos	10000	Celt2	Unlocked

ELBOW PADS

LEFT

Baller	Credits Required to Unlock	Baller	Credits Required to Unlock
White	Unlocked	Green	2,299
Red	2,299	Purple	2,299
Blue	2,299	Yellow	2,299
Black	2,299	Aqua	2,299

RIGHT

Baller	Credits Required to Unlock	Baller	Credits Required to Unlock
White	Unlocked	Green	2,299
Red	2,299	Purple	2,299
Blue	2,299	Yellow	2,299
Black	2,299	Aqua	2,299

BOTH

Baller	Credits Required to Unlock	Baller	Credits Required to Unlock
White	Unlocked	Green	2,299
Red	2,299	Purple	2,299
Blue	2,299	Yellow	2,299
Black	2,299	Aqua	2,299

WRIST GEAR

BRACELET - ROUND

Baller	Credits Required to Unlock	Baller	Credits Required to Unlock
Bronze	Unlocked	Gold	8,500
Silver	7,500		

BRACELET - WIDE

Baller	Credits Required to Unlock	Baller	Credits Required to Unlock
Bronze	Unlocked	Gold	8,500
Silver	7,500		

BRACELET - LINK

Baller	Credits Required to Unlock	Baller	Credits Required to Unlock
Bronze	Unlocked	Gold	8,500
Silver	7,500		

WRISTBAND - LEFT

Baller	Credits Required to Unlock	Baller	Credits Required to Unlock
Vanilla	Unlocked	True Blue	1500
Red Light	1500	Orange Peel	1500
True Blue	1500	Celtic Green	1500
Ambulance	1500	Buttah Blue	1500
Black	1500	Blue/White	2000
Teal	1500	Reggae	2350
Negative	1500	Americana	2350
Green	1500	Brake Light	2500
Purple	1500	Butta	2500
Grey	1500		

WRISTBAND - RIGHT

Baller	Credits Required to Unlock	Baller	Credits Required to Unlock
Vanilla	Unlocked	True Blue	1500
Red Light	1500	Orange Peel	1500
True Blue	1500	Celtic Green	1500
Ambulance	1500	Buttah Blue	1500
Black	1500	Blue/White	2000
Teal	1500	Reggae	2350
Negative	1500	Americana	2350
Green	1500	Brake Light	2500
Purple	1500	Butta	2500
Grey	1500		

WRISTBAND - BOTH

Baller	Credits Required to Unlock	Baller	Credits Required to Unlock
Vanilla	Unlocked	True Blue	1500
Red Light	1500	Orange Peel	1500
True Blue	1500	Celtic Green	1500
Ambulance	1500	Buttah Blue	1500
Black	1500	Blue/White	2000
Teal	1500	Reggae	2350
Negative	1500	Americana	2350
Green	1500	Brake Light	2500
Purple	1500	Butta	2500
Grey	1500		

WATCH

Baller	Credits Required to Unlock	Baller	Credits Required to Unlock
Gumball Machine	Unlocked	Calimanti	11,870
Night Hawk	Unlocked	Spoiler	12,599
Stealth Factor	Unlocked	Navigator	14,520
Fake Ice	1,594	Del Morato	15,300
Laser Storm	10,500	Larenzo	17,500
Focus	10,700		

BOTTOMS

JEANS

Baller	Credits Required to Unlock	Baller	Credits Required to Unlock
One Fine Ride	Unlocked	Patchwork	7,399
Faded	6,999	Division	7,544
Dark	7,000	Jungle Cammo	8,499
2 tone	7,299	Artic Cammo	8,499

NBA WARMUPS

Baller	Credits Required to Unlock	Baller	Credits Required to Unlock
Bobcats	5,500	Mavericks	5,500
Bucks	5,500	Nets	5,500
Bulls	5,500	Nuggets	5,500
Cavaliers	5,500	Pacers	5,500
Celtics	5,500	Pistons	5,500
Clippers	5,500	Raptors	5,500
Grizzlies	5,500	Rockets	5,500
Hawks	5,500	Sixers	5,500
Heat	5,500	Sonics	5,500
Hornets	5,500	Spurs	5,500
Jazz	5,500	Suns	5,500
Kings	5,500	Timberwolves	5,500
Knicks	5,500	Trail Blazers	5,500
Lakers	5,500	Warriors	5,500
Magic	5,500	Wizards	5,500

SHORTS

Baller	Credits Required to Unlock	Baller	Credits Required to Unlock
Bobcats	5,500	Hornets	5,500
Bucks	5,500	Jazz	5,500
Bulls	5,500	Kings	5,500
Cavaliers	5,500	Knicks	5,500
Celtics	5,500	Lakers	5,500
Classic Bullets	9,500	Magic	5,500
Classic Celtics	9,500	Mavericks	5,500
Classic Hawks	9,500	Nets	5,500
Classic Jazz	9,500	Nuggets	5,500
Classic Knicks	9,500	Pacers	5,500
Classic Lakers	9,500	Pistons	5,500
Classic Pistons	9,500	Raptors	5,500
Classic Royals	9,500	Rockets	5,500
Classic Sixers	9,500	Sixers	5,500
Classic Spurs	9,500	Sonics	5,500
Classic Trail Blazers	9,500	Spurs	5,500
Classic Trail Blazers Alt	9,500	Suns	5,500
Classic Warriors	9,500	Timberwolves	5,500
Clippers	5,500	Trail Blazers	5,500
Grizzlies	5,500	Warriors	5,500
Hawks	5,500	Wizards	5,500
Heat	5,500		

SHORTS (HIGH SOCKS)

Baller	Credits Required to Unlock	Baller	Credits Required to Unlock
Bobcats	5,500	Hornets	5,500
Bucks	5,500	Jazz	5,500
Bulls	5,500	Kings	5,500
Cavaliers	5,500	Knicks	5,500
Celtics	5,500	Lakers	5,500
Classic Bullets	9,500	Magic	5,500
Classic Celtics	9,500	Mavericks	5,500
Classic Hawks	9,500	Nets	5,500
Classic Jazz	9,500	Nuggets	5,500
Classic Knicks	9,500	Pacers	5,500
Classic Lakers	9,500	Pistons	5,500
Classic Pistons	9,500	Raptors	5,500
Classic Royals	9,500	Rockets	5,500
Classic Sixers	9,500	Sixers	5,500
Classic Spurs	9,500	Sonics	5,500
Classic Trail Blazers	9,500	Spurs	5,500
Classic Trail Blazers Alt	9,500	Suns	5,500
Classic Warriors	9,500	Timberwolves	5,500
Clippers	5,500	Trail Blazers	5,500
Grizzlies	5,500	Warriors	5,500
Hawks	5,500	Wizards	5,500
Heat	5,500		

SHORTS (HIGH SOCKS)

Baller	Credits Required to Unlock	Baller	Credits Required to Unlock
Bobcats	5,500	Classic Spurs	9,500
Bucks	5,500	Classic Trail Blazers	9,500
Bulls	5,500	Classic Trail Blazers Alt	9,500
Cavaliers	5,500	Classic Warriors	9,500
Celtics	5,500	Clippers	5,500
Classic Bullets	9,500	Grizzlies	5,500
Classic Celtics	9,500	Hawks	5,500
Classic Hawks	9,500	Heat	5,500
Classic Jazz	9,500	Hornets	5,500
Classic Knicks	9,500	Jazz	5,500
Classic Lakers	9,500	Kings	5,500
Classic Pistons	9,500	Knicks	5,500
Classic Royals	9,500	Lakers	5,500
Classic Sixers	9,500	Magic	5,500

SHORTS (HIGH SOCKS)

Baller	Credits Required to Unlock	Baller	Credits Required to Unlock
Mavericks	5,500	Sonics	5,500
Nets	5,500	Spurs	5,500
Nuggets	5,500	Suns	5,500
Pacers	5,500	Timberwolves	5,500
Pistons	5,500	Trail Blazers	5,500
Raptors	5,500	Warriors	5,500
Rockets	5,500	Wizards	5,500
Sixers	5,500		

SHORTS (LOW SOCKS)

Baller	Credits Required to Unlock	Baller	Credits Required to Unlock
Bobcats	5,500	Hornets	5,500
Bucks	5,500	Jazz	5,500
Bulls	5,500	Kings	5,500
Cavaliers	5,500	Knicks	5,500
Celtics	5,500	Lakers	5,500
Classic Bullets	9,500	Magic	5,500
Classic Celtics	9,500	Mavericks	5,500
Classic Hawks	9,500	Nets	5,500
Classic Jazz	9,500	Nuggets	5,500
Classic Knicks	9,500	Pacers	5,500
Classic Lakers	9,500	Pistons	5,500
Classic Pistons	9,500	Raptors	5,500
Classic Royals	9,500	Rockets	5,500
Classic Sixers	9,500	Sixers	5,500
Classic Spurs	9,500	Sonics	5,500
Classic Trail Blazers	9,500	Spurs	5,500
Classic Trail Blazers Alt	9,500	Suns	5,500
Classic Warriors	9,500	Timberwolves	5,500
Clippers	5,500	Trail Blazers	5,500
Grizzlies	5,500	Warriors	5,500
Hawks	5,500	Wizards	5,500
Heat	5,500		

SUIT PANTS

Baller	Credits Required to Unlock	Baller	Credits Required to Unlock
Flat	Unlocked	Grafics	7,500
Grazin'	7,500	Jalapeno	7,500
Icy Disposition	7,500	Westside	7,500
Tantilizin'	7,500	Creamcicle	7,500
Figures	7,500	JBaller's Lustrous	8,500
Doctor Is In	7,500	Double Agent	8,500
Keep It Clean	7,500	Suit's Suit	8,500

SWEAT PANTS

Baller	Credits Required to Unlock	Baller	Credits Required to Unlock
Standard Affairs	Unlocked	Sweaty Zeebras	6,500
Go Green Go	5,200	Midnight Run	7,599
Baby Powder	5,899		

SWEATS (LEG-UPS)

Baller	Credits Required to Unlock	Baller	Credits Required to Unlock
Standard Affairs	Unlocked	Sweaty Zeebras	6,500
Go Green Go	5,200	Midnight Run	7,599
Baby Powder	5,899		

WARM UP PANTS

Baller	Credits Required to Unlock	Baller	Credits Required to Unlock
White	Unlocked	Blue & Navy	7655
Bum-Bizzle	5500	Butta	7899
Aqua & Green	7466	Gray & Black	Unlocked
Black	7488		

KNEE PADS

LEFT

Baller	Credits Required to Unlock	Baller	Credits Required to Unlock
White	Unlocked	Green	3,350
Red	3,350	Purple	3,350
Blue	3,350	Yellow	3,350
Black	3,350	Aqua	3,350

RIGHT

Baller	Credits Required to Unlock	Baller	Credits Required to Unlock
White	Unlocked	Green	3,350
Red	3,350	Purple	3,350
Blue	3,350	Yellow	3,350
Black	3,350	Aqua	3,350

BOTH

Baller	Credits Required to Unlock	Baller	Credits Required to Unlock
White	Unlocked	Green	3,350
Red	3,350	Purple	3,350
Blue	3,350	Yellow	3,350
Black	3,350	Aqua	3,350

SHOES

ATHLETIC

Baller	Credits Required to Unlock	Baller	Credits Required to Unlock
Scootaz II	Unlocked	G West-siders	4626
Green Hogs	Unlocked	Assists	4644
J.B. Fictionals v2	Unlocked	Incineratas	4688
Blue Hogs	Unlocked	S-Dhupelias	4699
High Flyers	2588	T-Dog's	4866
RJ-Naegelers	2644	On Fires	4955
Consequence	2855	Black Chrome	4966
Night Owl IV	2988	Midnight Hogs	5366
Impact Playa	3255	Knutz	5388
G Dogs	3522	DT-SmallFonts	5399
Yellow Rios	3500	P-Lynn Dog-walkers	5433
Olive Rios	3500	See Ya	5650
Soarins	3575	T's Rhino	5688
J-Rivetts	3677	J-Vinators	5722
Blue Rios	3700	Murakamisans	5733
Grey Rios	3700	Celtics Legend	5786
Yeow!	3765	Kicking It	5799
M-Rubinators	3855	Octapuss	5843
JohnnyV's	3877	Yo Mama's Callin	6355
Bailey All-Nighters	3944	Voltaires	6599
Shocks + Struts	3999	Inta-ceptas	6877
Bring Its 7	4265	DSJ IX	7200
Dark Blue Hogs	4266	Red Hogs	Unlocked
Turnstylez	4500		

CASUAL

Baller	Credits Required to Unlock
Smoove	Unlocked
Dawgs	5,000
Viva Italiano	8,599
Black Licorice	9,000
White Lightnin'	10,522

HAIR/ HEADGEAR

SHORT CROP

Baller	Credits Required to Unlock	Baller	Credits Required to Unlock
Blonde	Unlocked	Brown Stripes	2,468
Brown	Unlocked	Blonde Fade	2,500
Brown Slice Fade	2,133	Brown Fade	2,500
Blonde Slice Fade	2,133	Franco Stripes	2,598
Blonde Stripes	2,468	Franco Fade	2,759

SKULLY

Baller	Credits Required to Unlock	Baller	Credits Required to Unlock
White	White	Purple	3,788
Grey	Grey	Blue	3,788
Blue	3,788	Black	3,788
Green	3,788	Teal	3,788
Red	3,788	Purple	3,788
Yellow	3,788	Nylon	4,000

VISOR

Baller	Credits Required to Unlock	Baller	Credits Required to Unlock
Grey	Unlocked	Yellow	6,000
Green	6,000	Black	6,000
Purple	6,000	Red	6,000
Blue	6,000	White Bread	6,577
Teal	6,000	5-0	7,500

VISOR (BACK)

Baller	Credits Required to Unlock	Baller	Credits Required to Unlock
Grey	Unlocked	Yellow	6,000
Green	6,000	Black	6,000
Purple	6,000	Red	6,000
Blue	6,000	White Bread	6,577
Teal	6,000	5-0	7,500

VISOR (BK-FLIP)

Baller	Credits Required to Unlock	Baller	Credits Required to Unlock
Grey	Unlocked	Yellow	6,000
Green	6,000	Black	6,000
Purple	6,000	Red	6,000
Blue	6,000	White Bread	6,577
Teal	6,000	5-0	7,500

VISOR (LEFT)

Baller	Credits Required to Unlock	Baller	Credits Required to Unlock
Grey	Unlocked	Yellow	6,000
Green	6,000	Black	6,000
Purple	6,000	Red	6,000
Blue	6,000	White Bread	6,577
Teal	6,000	5-0	7,500

VISOR (RIGHT)

Baller	Credits Required to Unlock	Baller	Credits Required to Unlock
Grey	Unlocked	Yellow	6,000
Green	6,000	Black	6,000
Purple	6,000	Red	6,000
Blue	6,000	White Bread	6,577
Teal	6,000	5-0	7,500

AFRO-COMBO

Baller	Credits Required to Unlock	Baller	Credits Required to Unlock
Afro & Whitebread	Unlocked	Afro & Americana	6,977
Afro & Orange Peel	6,344	Afro & Blue/White	7,244

AFRO-COMBO (PICK)

Baller	Credits Required to Unlock	Baller	Credits Required to Unlock
Afro & Whitebread	Unlocked	Afro & Americana	6,977
Afro & Orange Peel	6,344	Afro & Blue/White	7,244

AFRO- LARGE

Baller	Credits Required to Unlock	Baller	Credits Required to Unlock
Afro	Unlocked	Cha Cha Cha Afro	5,495
Butta Fro	Unlocked	Red Haid	5,499
Purple Haid	5,489		

AFRO-COMBO- MEDIUM

Baller	Credits Required to Unlock	Baller	Credits Required to Unlock
Afro	Unlocked	Cha Cha Cha Afro	5,495
Butta Fro	Unlocked	Red Haid	5,499
Purple Haid	5,489		

AFRO-COMBO-SMALL

Baller	Credits Required to Unlock	Baller	Credits Required to Unlock
Afro	Unlocked	Cha Cha Cha Afro	5,495
Butta Fro	Unlocked	Red Haid	5,499
Purple Haid	5,489		

BANDANA

Baller	Credits Required to Unlock	Baller	Credits Required to Unlock
White	Unlocked	Teal	3,399
Grey	Unlocked	Blue	3,399
Purple	3,399	Red	3,399
Yellow	3,399	Camo	4,588
Green	3,399	Flaming	4,999
Black	3,399		

BANDANA (BACK)

Baller	Credits Required to Unlock	Baller	Credits Required to Unlock
White	Unlocked	Teal	3,399
Grey	Unlocked	Blue	3,399
Purple	3,399	Red	3,399
Yellow	3,399	Camo	4,588
Green	3,399	Flaming	4,999
Black	3,399		

BANDANA (FOLDED)

Baller	Credits Required to Unlock	Baller	Credits Required to Unlock
White	Unlocked	Teal	3,399
Grey	Unlocked	Orange	3,399
Purple	3,399	Blue	3,399
Yellow	3,399	Red	3,399
Green	3,399	Camo	4,588
Black	3,399		

BEANIE

Baller	Credits Required to Unlock	Baller	Credits Required to Unlock
White	Unlocked	Yellow	3,564
Grey	Unlocked	Orange	3,564
Green	3,564	Indigo	3,564
Purple	3,564	Red	3,564
Blue	3,564	Nice	4,500
Teal	3,564	Black & White	4,500
Black	3,564	Red & White Beanie	4,529

BUCKET

Baller	Credits Required to Unlock	Baller	Credits Required to Unlock
Plain	Unlocked	Purple	5,500
Green	5,500	White	5,500
Red	5,500	Blue Striped	5,999
Blue	5,500	Camo	6,050
Yellow	5,500	Night	7,323
Teal	5,500	Red Stripe Night	7,599

CAP

Baller	Credits Required to Unlock	Baller	Credits Required to Unlock
Criterion	Unlocked	Sonics	6,000
Midway	Unlocked	Celtics	6,000
Kanji	5,433	Cavs	6,000
Pacers	6,000	Grizzlies	6,000
Nuggets	6,000	Clippers	6,000
Raptors	6,000	Bucks	6,000
Pistons	6,000	Blazers	6,000
Magic	6,000	Bulls	6,000
Lakers	6,000	Kings	6,000
Nets	6,000	Jazz	6,000
Mavericks	6,000	Knicks	6,000
Warriors	6,000	Heat	6,000
Suns	6,000	Hawks	6,000
Timberwolves	6,000	Hornets	6,000
Wizards	6,000	Blue Star	7,466
Sixers	6,000	BullDawg	7,899
Rockets	6,000	Ballers	8,000
Spurs	6,000		

CAP (BACK)

Baller	Credits Required to Unlock	Baller	Credits Required to Unlock
Criterion	Unlocked	Sonics	6,000
Midway	Unlocked	Celtics	6,000
Kanji	5,433	Cavs	6,000
Pacers	6,000	Grizzlies	6,000
Nuggets	6,000	Clippers	6,000
Raptors	6,000	Bucks	6,000
Pistons	6,000	Blazers	6,000
Magic	6,000	Bulls	6,000
Lakers	6,000	Kings	6,000
Nets	6,000	Jazz	6,000
Mavericks	6,000	Knicks	6,000
Warriors	6,000	Heat	6,000
Suns	6,000	Hawks	6,000
Timberwolves	6,000	Hornets	6,000
Wizards	6,000	Blue Star	7,466
Sixers	6,000	BullDawg	7,899
Rockets	6,000	Ballers	8,000
Spurs	6,000		

CAP (BK-LT)

Baller	Credits Required to Unlock	Baller	Credits Required to Unlock
Criterion	Unlocked	Sonics	6,000
Midway	Unlocked	Celtics	6,000
Kanji	5,433	Cavs	6,000
Pacers	6,000	Grizzlies	6,000
Nuggets	6,000	Clippers	6,000
Raptors	6,000	Bucks	6,000
Pistons	6,000	Blazers	6,000
Magic	6,000	Bulls	6,000
Lakers	6,000	Kings	6,000
Nets	6,000	Jazz	6,000
Mavericks	6,000	Knicks	6,000
Warriors	6,000	Heat	6,000
Suns	6,000	Hawks	6,000
Timberwolves	6,000	Hornets	6,000
Wizards	6,000	Blue Star	7,466
Sixers	6,000	BullDawg	7,899
Rockets	6,000	Ballers	8,000
Spurs	6,000		

CAP (BK-RT)

Baller	Credits Required to Unlock	Baller	Credits Required to Unlock
Criterion	Unlocked	Sonics	6,000
Midway	Unlocked	Celtics	6,000
Kanji	5,433	Cavs	6,000
Pacers	6,000	Grizzlies	6,000
Nuggets	6,000	Clippers	6,000
Raptors	6,000	Bucks	6,000
Pistons	6,000	Blazers	6,000
Magic	6,000	Bulls	6,000
Lakers	6,000	Kings	6,000
Nets	6,000	Jazz	6,000
Mavericks	6,000	Knicks	6,000
Warriors	6,000	Heat	6,000
Suns	6,000	Hawks	6,000
Timberwolves	6,000	Hornets	6,000
Wizards	6,000	Blue Star	7,466
Sixers	6,000	BullDawg	7,899
Rockets	6,000	Ballers	8,000
Spurs	6,000		

CAP (LEFT)

Baller	Credits Required to Unlock	Baller	Credits Required to Unlock
Criterion	Unlocked	Sonics	6,000
Midway	Unlocked	Celtics	6,000
Kanji	5,433	Cavs	6,000
Pacers	6,000	Grizzlies	6,000
Nuggets	6,000	Clippers	6,000
Raptors	6,000	Bucks	6,000
Pistons	6,000	Blazers	6,000
Magic	6,000	Bulls	6,000
Lakers	6,000	Kings	6,000
Nets	6,000	Jazz	6,000
Mavericks	6,000	Knicks	6,000
Warriors	6,000	Heat	6,000
Suns	6,000	Hawks	6,000
Timberwolves	6,000	Hornets	6,000
Wizards	6,000	Blue Star	7,466
Sixers	6,000	BullDawg	7,899
Rockets	6,000	Ballers	8,000
Spurs	6,000		

CAP (RIGHT)

Baller	Credits Required to Unlock	Baller	Credits Required to Unlock
Criterion	Unlocked	Sonics	6,000
Midway	Unlocked	Celtics	6,000
Kanji	5,433	Cavs	6,000
Pacers	6,000	Grizzlies	6,000
Nuggets	6,000	Clippers	6,000
Raptors	6,000	Bucks	6,000
Pistons	6,000	Blazers	6,000
Magic	6,000	Bulls	6,000
Lakers	6,000	Kings	6,000
Nets	6,000	Jazz	6,000
Mavericks	6,000	Knicks	6,000
Warriors	6,000	Heat	6,000
Suns	6,000	Hawks	6,000
Timberwolves	6,000	Hornets	6,000
Wizards	6,000	Blue Star	7,466
Sixers	6,000	BullDawg	7,899
Rockets	6,000	Ballers	8,000
Spurs	6,000		

CAP-COMBO

Baller	Credits Required to Unlock	Baller	Credits Required to Unlock
Criterion	Unlocked	Nets	6,000
Midway	Unlocked	Mavericks	6,000
Kanji	5,433	Warriors	6,000
Pacers	6,000	Suns	6,000
Nuggets	6,000	Timberwolves	6,000
Raptors	6,000	Wizards	6,000
Pistons	6,000	Sixers	6,000
Magic	6,000	Rockets	6,000
Lakers	6,000	Spurs	6,000

CAP- COMBO (CONTINUED)

Baller	Credits Required to Unlock	Baller	Credits Required to Unlock
Sonics	6,000	Jazz	6,000
Celtics	6,000	Knicks	6,000
Cavs	6,000	Heat	6,000
Grizzlies	6,000	Hawks	6,000
Clippers	6,000	Hornets	6,000
Bucks	6,000	Blue Star	7,466
Blazers	6,000	BullDawg	7,899
Bulls	6,000	Ballers	8,000
Kings	6,000		

CAP- COMBO (BK)

Baller	Credits Required to Unlock	Baller	Credits Required to Unlock
Criterion	Unlocked	Sonics	6,000
Midway	Unlocked	Celtics	6,000
Kanji	5,433	Cavs	6,000
Pacers	6,000	Grizzlies	6,000
Nuggets	6,000	Clippers	6,000
Raptors	6,000	Bucks	6,000
Pistons	6,000	Blazers	6,000
Magic	6,000	Bulls	6,000
Lakers	6,000	Kings	6,000
Nets	6,000	Jazz	6,000
Mavericks	6,000	Knicks	6,000
Warriors	6,000	Heat	6,000
Suns	6,000	Hawks	6,000
Timberwolves	6,000	Hornets	6,000
Wizards	6,000	Blue Star	7,466
Sixers	6,000	BullDawg	7,899
Rockets	6,000	Ballers	8,000
Spurs	6,000		

CAP- COMBO (LI)

Baller	Credits Required to Unlock	Baller	Credits Required to Unlock
Criterion	Unlocked	Nuggets	6,000
Midway	Unlocked	Raptors	6,000
Kanji	5,433	Pistons	6,000
Pacers	6,000	Magic	6,000

CAP- COMBO (LT)

Baller	Credits Required to Unlock	Baller	Credits Required to Unlock
Lakers	6,000	Clippers	6,000
Nets	6,000	Bucks	6,000
Mavericks	6,000	Blazers	6,000
Warriors	6,000	Bulls	6,000
Suns	6,000	Kings	6,000
Timberwolves	6,000	Jazz	6,000
Wizards	6,000	Knicks	6,000
Sixers	6,000	Heat	6,000
Rockets	6,000	Hawks	6,000
Spurs	6,000	Hornets	6,000
Sonics	6,000	Blue Star	7,466
Celtics	6,000	BullDawg	7,899
Cavs	6,000	Ballers	8,000
Grizzlies	6,000		

CAP- COMBO (BK)

Baller	Credits Required to Unlock	Baller	Credits Required to Unlock
Criterion	Unlocked	Timberwolves	6,000
Midway	Unlocked	Wizards	6,000
Kanji	5,433	Sixers	6,000
Pacers	6,000	Rockets	6,000
Nuggets	6,000	Spurs	6,000
Raptors	6,000	Sonics	6,000
Pistons	6,000	Celtics	6,000
Magic	6,000	Cavs	6,000
Lakers	6,000	Grizzlies	6,000
Nets	6,000	Clippers	6,000
Mavericks	6,000	Bucks	6,000
Warriors	6,000	Blazers	6,000
Suns	6,000	Bulls	6,000

CAP-COMBO (BK) -CONTINUED

Baller	Credits Required to Unlock	Baller	Credits Required to Unlock
Kings	6,000	Hornets	6,000
Jazz	6,000	Blue Star	7,466
Knicks	6,000	BullDawg	7,899
Heat	6,000	Ballers	8,000
Hawks	6,000		

CAP-FLAT

Baller	Credits Required to Unlock	Baller	Credits Required to Unlock
Criterion	Unlocked	Sonics	6,000
Midway	Unlocked	Celtics	6,000
Kanji	5,433	Cavs	6,000
Pacers	6,000	Grizzlies	6,000
Nuggets	6,000	Clippers	6,000
Raptors	6,000	Bucks	6,000
Pistons	6,000	Blazers	6,000
Magic	6,000	Bulls	6,000
Lakers	6,000	Kings	6,000
Nets	6,000	Jazz	6,000
Mavericks	6,000	Knicks	6,000
Warriors	6,000	Heat	6,000
Suns	6,000	Hawks	6,000
Timberwolves	6,000	Hornets	6,000
Wizards	6,000	Blue Star	7,466
Sixers	6,000	BullDawg	7,899
Rockets	6,000	Ballers	8,000
Spurs	6,000		

CAP-FLAT BACK

Baller	Credits Required to Unlock	Baller	Credits Required to Unlock
Criterion	Unlocked	Raptors	6,000
Midway	Unlocked	Pistons	6,000
Kanji	5,433	Magic	6,000
Pacers	6,000	Lakers	6,000
Nuggets	6,000	Nets	6,000

CAP- FLAT BACK (CONTINUED)

Baller	Credits Required to Unlock	Baller	Credits Required to Unlock
Mavericks	6,000	Bucks	6,000
Warriors	6,000	Blazers	6,000
Suns	6,000	Bulls	6,000
Timberwolves	6,000	Kings	6,000
Wizards	6,000	Jazz	6,000
Sixers	6,000	Knicks	6,000
Rockets	6,000	Heat	6,000
Spurs	6,000	Hawks	6,000
Sonics	6,000	Hornets	6,000
Celtics	6,000	Blue Star	7,466
Cavs	6,000	BullDawg	7,899
Grizzlies	6,000	Ballers	8,000
Clippers	6,000		

CAP- FLAT (BACK - LT)

Baller	Credits Required to Unlock	Baller	Credits Required to Unlock
Criterion	Unlocked	Sixers	6,000
Midway	Unlocked	Rockets	6,000
Kanji	5,433	Spurs	6,000
Pacers	6,000	Sonics	6,000
Nuggets	6,000	Celtics	6,000
Raptors	6,000	Cavs	6,000
Pistons	6,000	Grizzlies	6,000
Magic	6,000	Clippers	6,000
Lakers	6,000	Bucks	6,000
Nets	6,000	Blazers	6,000
Mavericks	6,000	Bulls	6,000
Warriors	6,000	Kings	6,000
Suns	6,000	Jazz	6,000
Timberwolves	6,000	Knicks	6,000
Wizards	6,000	Heat	6,000

CAP-FLAT (BACK-LT)-CONTINUED

Baller	Credits Required to Unlock	Baller	Credits Required to Unlock
Hawks	6,000	BullDawg	7,899
Hornets	6,000	Ballers	8,000
Blue Star	7,466		

CAP-FLAT (BACK-RT)

Baller	Credits Required to Unlock	Baller	Credits Required to Unlock
Criterion	Unlocked	Sonics	6,000
Midway	Unlocked	Celtics	6,000
Kanji	5,433	Cavs	6,000
Pacers	6,000	Grizzlies	6,000
Nuggets	6,000	Clippers	6,000
Raptors	6,000	Bucks	6,000
Pistons	6,000	Blazers	6,000
Magic	6,000	Bulls	6,000
Lakers	6,000	Kings	6,000
Nets	6,000	Jazz	6,000
Mavericks	6,000	Knicks	6,000
Warriors	6,000	Heat	6,000
Suns	6,000	Hawks	6,000
Timberwolves	6,000	Hornets	6,000
Wizards	6,000	Blue Star	7,466
Sixers	6,000	BullDawg	7,899
Rockets	6,000	Ballers	8,000
Spurs	6,000		

CAP- FLAT (LEFT)

Baller	Credits Required to Unlock	Baller	Credits Required to Unlock
Criterion	Unlocked	Sonics	6,000
Midway	Unlocked	Celtics	6,000
Kanji	5,433	Cavs	6,000
Pacers	6,000	Grizzlies	6,000
Nuggets	6,000	Clippers	6,000
Raptors	6,000	Bucks	6,000
Pistons	6,000	Blazers	6,000
Magic	6,000	Bulls	6,000
Lakers	6,000	Kings	6,000
Nets	6,000	Jazz	6,000
Mavericks	6,000	Knicks	6,000
Warriors	6,000	Heat	6,000
Suns	6,000	Hawks	6,000
Timberwolves	6,000	Hornets	6,000
Wizards	6,000	Blue Star	7,466
Sixers	6,000	BullDawg	7,899
Rockets	6,000	Ballers	8,000
Spurs	6,000		

CAP-FLAT (RIGHT)

Baller	Credits Required to Unlock	Baller	Credits Required to Unlock
Criterion	Unlocked	Nets	6,000
Midway	Unlocked	Mavericks	6,000
Kanji	5,433	Warriors	6,000
Pacers	6,000	Suns	6,000
Nuggets	6,000	Timberwolves	6,000
Raptors	6,000	Wizards	6,000
Pistons	6,000	Sixers	6,000
Magic	6,000	Rockets	6,000
Lakers	6,000	Spurs	6,000

CAP- FLAT (RIGHT) - CONTINUED

Baller	Credits Required to Unlock	Baller	Credits Required to Unlock
Sonics	6,000	Jazz	6,000
Celtics	6,000	Knicks	6,000
Cavs	6,000	Heat	6,000
Grizzlies	6,000	Hawks	6,000
Clippers	6,000	Hornets	6,000
Bucks	6,000	Blue Star	7,466
Blazers	6,000	BullDawg	7,899
Bulls	6,000	Ballers	8,000
Kings	6,000		

CAP- FLAT (COMBO)

Baller	Credits Required to Unlock	Baller	Credits Required to Unlock
Criterion	Unlocked	Sonics	6,000
Midway	Unlocked	Celtics	6,000
Kanji	5,433	Cavs	6,000
Pacers	6,000	Grizzlies	6,000
Nuggets	6,000	Clippers	6,000
Raptors	6,000	Bucks	6,000
Pistons	6,000	Blazers	6,000
Magic	6,000	Bulls	6,000
Lakers	6,000	Kings	6,000
Nets	6,000	Jazz	6,000
Mavericks	6,000	Knicks	6,000
Warriors	6,000	Heat	6,000
Suns	6,000	Hawks	6,000
Timberwolves	6,000	Hornets	6,000
Wizards	6,000	Blue Star	7,466
Sixers	6,000	BullDawg	7,899
Rockets	6,000	Ballers	8,000
Spurs	6,000		

CAP-SMALL

Baller	Credits Required to Unlock	Baller	Credits Required to Unlock
Criterion	Unlocked	Sonics	6,000
Midway	Unlocked	Celtics	6,000
Kanji	5,433	Cavs	6,000
Pacers	6,000	Grizzlies	6,000
Nuggets	6,000	Clippers	6,000
Raptors	6,000	Bucks	6,000
Pistons	6,000	Blazers	6,000
Magic	6,000	Bulls	6,000
Lakers	6,000	Kings	6,000
Nets	6,000	Jazz	6,000
Mavericks	6,000	Knicks	6,000
Warriors	6,000	Heat	6,000
Suns	6,000	Hawks	6,000
Timberwolves	6,000	Hornets	6,000
Wizards	6,000	Blue Star	7,466
Sixers	6,000	BullDawg	7,899
Rockets	6,000	Ballers	8,000
Spurs	6,000		

CORNROWS

Baller	Credits Required to Unlock
Cornrows	Unlocked

DO-RAG

Baller	Credits Required to Unlock	Baller	Credits Required to Unlock
White	Unlocked	Teal	4,855
Grey	Unlocked	Red	4,855
Purple	4,855	Orange	4,855
Yellow	4,855	Blue	4,855
Green	4,855	Leopold	5,999
Black	4,855	Cannonball	5,999

FEDORA

Baller	Credits Required to Unlock	Baller	Credits Required to Unlock
White	Unlocked	Mr. Jones	9,399
Straw-Blueband	9,099	Classic Black	9,455
Hot Pink	9,199	All Blue	9,468
Camo	9,255	White-Redband	9,500

FLAT-COMBO (BK)

Baller	Credits Required to Unlock	Baller	Credits Required to Unlock
Criterion	Unlocked	Sonics	6,000
Midway	Unlocked	Celtics	6,000
Kanji	5,433	Cavs	6,000
Pacers	6,000	Grizzlies	6,000
Nuggets	6,000	Clippers	6,000
Raptors	6,000	Bucks	6,000
Pistons	6,000	Blazers	6,000
Magic	6,000	Bulls	6,000
Lakers	6,000	Kings	6,000
Nets	6,000	Jazz	6,000
Mavericks	6,000	Knicks	6,000
Warriors	6,000	Heat	6,000
Suns	6,000	Hawks	6,000
Timberwolves	6,000	Hornets	6,000
Wizards	6,000	Blue Star	7,466
Sixers	6,000	BullDawg	7,899
Rockets	6,000	Ballers	8,000
Spurs	6,000		

FLAT-COMBO (BK-LT)

Baller	Credits Required to Unlock	Baller	Credits Required to Unlock
Criterion	Unlocked	Nets	6,000
Midway	Unlocked	Mavericks	6,000
Kanji	5,433	Warriors	6,000
Pacers	6,000	Suns	6,000
Nuggets	6,000	Timberwolves	6,000
Raptors	6,000	Wizards	6,000
Pistons	6,000	Sixers	6,000
Magic	6,000	Rockets	6,000
Lakers	6,000	Spurs	6,000

FLAT-COMBO (BK-IT) - CONTINUED

Baller	Credits Required to Unlock	Baller	Credits Required to Unlock
Sonics	6,000	Jazz	6,000
Celtics	6,000	Knicks	6,000
Cavs	6,000	Heat	6,000
Grizzlies	6,000	Hawks	6,000
Clippers	6,000	Hornets	6,000
Bucks	6,000	Blue Star	7,466
Blazers	6,000	BullDawg	7,899
Bulls	6,000	Ballers	8,000
Kings	6,000		

FLAT-COMBO (BK-RT)

Baller	Credits Required to Unlock	Baller	Credits Required to Unlock
Criterion	Unlocked	Sonics	6,000
Midway	Unlocked	Celtics	6,000
Kanji	5,433	Cavs	6,000
Pacers	6,000	Grizzlies	6,000
Nuggets	6,000	Clippers	6,000
Raptors	6,000	Bucks	6,000
Pistons	6,000	Blazers	6,000
Magic	6,000	Bulls	6,000
Lakers	6,000	Kings	6,000
Nets	6,000	Jazz	6,000
Mavericks	6,000	Knicks	6,000
Warriors	6,000	Heat	6,000
Suns	6,000	Hawks	6,000
Timberwolves	6,000	Hornets	6,000
Wizards	6,000	Blue Star	7,466
Sixers	6,000	BullDawg	7,899
Rockets	6,000	Ballers	8,000
Spurs	6,000		

FLAT-COMBO (LT)

Baller	Credits Required to Unlock	Baller	Credits Required to Unlock
Criterion	Unlocked	Sonics	6,000
Midway	Unlocked	Celtics	6,000
Kanji	5,433	Cavs	6,000
Pacers	6,000	Grizzlies	6,000
Nuggets	6,000	Clippers	6,000
Raptors	6,000	Bucks	6,000
Pistons	6,000	Blazers	6,000
Magic	6,000	Bulls	6,000
Lakers	6,000	Kings	6,000
Nets	6,000	Jazz	6,000
Mavericks	6,000	Knicks	6,000
Warriors	6,000	Heat	6,000
Suns	6,000	Hawks	6,000
Timberwolves	6,000	Hornets	6,000
Wizards	6,000	Blue Star	7,466
Sixers	6,000	BullDawg	7,899
Rockets	6,000	Ballers	8,000
Spurs	6,000		

FLAT-COMBO (RT)

Baller	Credits Required to Unlock	Baller	Credits Required to Unlock
Criterion	Unlocked	Nets	6,000
Midway	Unlocked	Mavericks	6,000
Kanji	5,433	Warriors	6,000
Pacers	6,000	Suns	6,000
Nuggets	6,000	Timberwolves	6,000
Raptors	6,000	Wizards	6,000
Pistons	6,000	Sixers	6,000
Magic	6,000	Rockets	6,000
Lakers	6,000	Spurs	6,000

FLAT-COMBO (RT) - CONTINUED

Baller	Credits Required to Unlock	Baller	Credits Required to Unlock
Sonics	6,000	Jazz	6,000
Celtics	6,000	Knicks	6,000
Cavs	6,000	Heat	6,000
Grizzlies	6,000	Hawks	6,000
Clippers	6,000	Hornets	6,000
Bucks	6,000	Blue Star	7,466
Blazers	6,000	BullDawg	7,899
Bulls	6,000	Ballers	8,000
Kings	6,000		

FLATTOP - LONG

Baller	Credits Required to Unlock	Baller	Credits Required to Unlock
Blonde	Unlocked	Brown Strips	2,468
Brown	Unlocked	Blonde Fade	2,500
Brown Slice Fade	2,133	Brown Fade	2,500
Blonde Slice Fade	2,133	Franco Stripes	2,598
Blonde Stripes	2,468	Franco Fade	2,759

FLATTOP - MEDIUM

Baller	Credits Required to Unlock	Baller	Credits Required to Unlock
Blonde	Unlocked	Brown Strips	2,468
Brown	Unlocked	Blonde Fade	2,500
Brown Slice Fade	2,133	Brown Fade	2,500
Blonde Slice Fade	2,133	Franco Stripes	2,598
Blonde Stripes	2,468	Franco Fade	2,759

FLATTOP - SHORT

Baller	Credits Required to Unlock	Baller	Credits Required to Unlock
Blonde	Unlocked	Brown Strips	2,468
Brown	Unlocked	Blonde Fade	2,500
Brown Slice Fade	2,133	Brown Fade	2,500
Blonde Slice Fade	2,133	Franco Stripes	2,598
Blonde Stripes	2,468	Franco Fade	2,759

HAIR - MEDIUM

Baller	Credits Required to Unlock	Baller	Credits Required to Unlock
Brown Flashback	Unlocked	Red Flashback	5,500
Black Flashback	Unlocked	Purple Flashback	5,500
Blonde Flashback	2,500	Green Flashback	5,500
Blue Flashback	5,500		

HAIR - PARTED

Baller	Credits Required to Unlock	Baller	Credits Required to Unlock
Booty Cutt	Unlocked	Too Much Fiber Cut	1,500
Bayside	1,500	Not My Real Hair	5,500
Brown part	1,500	Art Major	5,500

HEADBAND

Baller	Credits Required to Unlock	Baller	Credits Required to Unlock
White	Unlocked	Yellow	2,500
Grey	Unlocked	Red Light	2,500
Purple	2,500	Orange Peel	2,500
Green	2,500	True Blue	2,500
Teal	2,500	Americana	3,200
Negative	2,500	Blue & White	3,500

JAZZE' CAP

Baller	Credits Required to Unlock	Baller	Credits Required to Unlock
Purple	Unlocked	Blue Crushed	4,599
Grey	Unlocked	Red Crushed	4,599
Green Blue	4,599	Purple Crushed	4,599
Blue	4,599	Red	4,599
Teal	4,599	White	4,599
Black	4,599	Celtic Crushed	5,212
Yellow	4,599		

PAPER BOY

Baller	Credits Required to Unlock	Baller	Credits Required to Unlock
Black	Unlocked	Yellow	5,889
Plain	Unlocked	Orange	5,889
Green	5,889	Red	5,889
Purple	5,889	White	6,244
Blue	5,889	Leather	6,499
Teal	5,889	Race Car	6,500

GLASSES

RELAX

Baller	Credits Required to Unlock	Baller	Credits Required to Unlock
Sea Shade	Unlocked	Knox	6,499
GranPa	5,233	GranMa	7,320
Rosies	5,899	Peachy Pink	7,321

RELAX

Baller	Credits Required to Unlock	Baller	Credits Required to Unlock
Hexadecimals	Unlocked	L7	7,000
Tastemaker	5,873	Buttah Snaps	7,544
Quests	6,500	Swingers	7,653
Gold Rush	7,000		

ROUND

Baller	Credits Required to Unlock	Baller	Credits Required to Unlock
Blue Steel	Unlocked	Hard Drive	3,799
Led Sled	3,650	Solar Gold	4,853
Supercharged	3,651	Gqizzle	5,587

STYLIN'

Baller	Credits Required to Unlock	Baller	Credits Required to Unlock
Ramzul's A-Nerd	Unlocked	Snowflakes	5,599
Frosted	Unlocked	Katana	6,500
Crusaders	Unlocked	Black	7,000
Brass Key	5,500		

BEACH

Baller	Credits Required to Unlock	Baller	Credits Required to Unlock
Blanco	Unlocked	Sea Tortoise	6855
Image Tools	5788	White On Rice	7000
Tortoise	6099	Nightshade	7455
Attosecs	6777		

CASUAL

Baller	Credits Required to Unlock	Baller	Credits Required to Unlock
Cazualities	Unlocked	Cool Guy	6100
Jess'izzles	5099	Tree Tiger	6233
Chizzles	5399	Silvers	7500

DIAMOND

Baller	Credits Required to Unlock	Baller	Credits Required to Unlock
Bishops	Unlocked	Green Clover	8,522
Cruisin'	7,400	Tasty Freeze	8,655
Thrilla'Vanilla	7,599	Purple Haze	8,777
Blue Krush	7,999	Fantastical	8,999
Ice and Dice	8,122	Mango Tango	9,599

FLYBOY

Baller	Credits Required to Unlock	Baller	Credits Required to Unlock
Diablo Purple	Unlocked	Shark Bait	5,496
Red Moon Rising	5,295	Slash O Purple	5,995
Bobcat Orange	5,475	Flyboy	6,378

GOGGLES

Baller	Credits Required to Unlock	Baller	Credits Required to Unlock
Standard	Unlocked	Purple	5,000
Green	5,000	Blue	5,000
Red	5,000	Silver	5,000

METAL

Baller	Credits Required to Unlock	Baller	Credits Required to Unlock
Aces	Unlocked	Trans to Seq	5,322
Testify	5,000	Wireframes	5,688
Rock & Red	5,155	Hossy	7,655

NERD

Baller	Credits Required to Unlock	Baller	Credits Required to Unlock
Programmahz	Unlocked	Algies	5,899
Crackers	5,144	4-Eyes	6,122
X-Rays	5,422	Broken Windows	7,999

FACIAL HAIR

Baller	Credits Required to Unlock	Baller	Credits Required to Unlock
Scruff	Unlocked	Fu Man Chu	Unlocked
Chops	Unlocked	Chinstrap	Unlocked
Stripe	Unlocked	Clean Shave	Unlocked
Thin 'stache	Unlocked	Must Have A	Unlocked
Treasure Trail	Unlocked	Goatee	Unlocked

ACQUIRE A CRIB

Use your credit to unlock new homes as you progress through the game. You will notice that some cribs will already be unlocked from the start of the game.

THE DUNCAN FAMILY COMPOUND

This beautiful oceanfront estate is inspired by Italian Renaissance architecture.
credits required: Unlocked

THE MARBURY RESIDENCE

A 1000 ft. game room and a sport court featuring a custom perimeter cooling system are just a couple features of this astonishing home.
credits required: Unlocked

THE GARNETT RESIDENCE

Surrounded by natural waterfalls, this home has been designed to blend into the nearby environmental features. credits required: Unlocked

HOLCOMBE RUCKER PLAYGROUND

One of the most famous street ball courts in the world, this playground is frequented by local legends and baller idols. credits required: Unlocked

ALLEN IVERSON'S STUDIO 3

This well known studio, which has produced some of hip-hop's best known work, surrounds a basketball court and is covered by a hemispherical, basketball-shaped domed skylight roof.
Credits required: 1,250,000

THE KIDD FAMILY ESTATE

This 10,000 square ft. mansion has a backyard surrounded by water features.
Credits required: 1,250,000

THE O'NEAL RESIDENCE

This huge 15,000 square ft. LA home features views of the city and a garage with room for 20 cars.
Credits required: 1,500,000

THE MALONES' WINTER CHALET

With a stunning view of the snowy mountains, this home was heavily influenced by European ski traditions.
Credits required: 1,500,000

THE FRANCIS HOME-GALVESTON BAY ESTATES

This 6500 square ft. estate features carrera marble-faced, monolithic waterfalls.
Credits required: 1,750,000

THE BRYANT VACATION VILLA

This 15th century villa surrounded by olive groves is a great place for Kobe to kick up his heels.
Credits required: 2,000,000

VC'S PINNACLE TOWER PENTHOUSE

This fantastic suite overlooking the city of Toronto is equipped with a helipad and stone sculptures designed by neo-realist sculptor "JT".
Credits required: 2,500,000

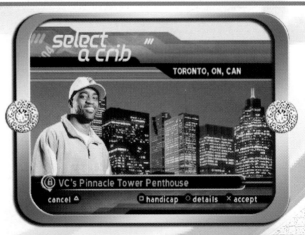

THE MCGRADY MANOR

Custom-built for T-Mac himself, this impressive estate has backyard access to an 18-hole championship golf course.
Credits required: 2,500,000

SCOTTIE PIPPEN'S YACHT

This 91 meter Tsunami class sport Yacht can propel seaward Scottie with four 2000hp Hydromarine Turbines.
Credits required: 2,700,000

THE PREPARATORY ACADEMY

Featuring an intense training curriculum, the Preparatory Academy has been home to many of China's greats.
Credits required: 3,000,000

GARAGE

Ready for a new ride? Go ahead-indulge yourself and enter the garage. Use the L and R buttons to cycle through the different models, then use the directional pad to choose a color.

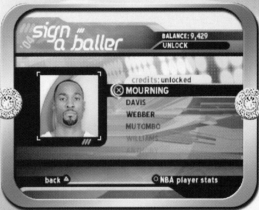

Cars	Available Colors	Credits Required to Unlock
Range Rover	Black, Blue, Green, Grey	300,000
Escudo	Blue, Green, Red, Yellow	75,000
Tigre	Grey, Black, Silver, Yellow	200,000
XLR Roadster	Silver, Black, Grey, Red	275,000
Escalade	Silver, Red, White, Blue	300,000
Dakkar	Green, Grey, Orange, Red	100,000
Interceptor	Blue, Red, Yellow, Grey	275,000
Transtusik	Yellow, Silver, Black, Blue	150,000

COLLECTIBLES

Unlock Magazines, Friends, Big Shots, and some other special Midway treats by performing specific objectives during play. Highlight an item in a folder to see what is required to unlock an object.

MAGAZINES

#	Required to Unlock	Desription
1	Play 25 matches on one profile	The cover of the August 2002 issue of NBA Inside Stuff magazine. Issue highlights include the top 16 photos of the season and T-Mac is interviewed and labeled the NBA's next bona fide superstar.
2	Play 50 matches on one profile	The cover of the January 1995 issue of NBA Inside Stuff magazine.
3	Play 75 matches on one profile	The cover of February 2002 issue of Hoop magazine.
4	Play 100 matches on one profile	The cover of the April 1998 issue of Hoop magazine.
5	Play 200 matches on one profile	The cover of the May 1998 issue of NBA Inside Stuff magazine.
6	Win 10 matches on one profile	The cover of the February 1996 issue of NBA Inside Stuff magazine.
7	30 matches on one profile	The cover of the January 1999 issue of NBA Inside Stuff magazine. In this issue P. Ewing and K. Johnson recall their first NBA games, Doug Christie talks about defending the 2-On-1 fast break and LaPhonso Ellis speaks on K. Malone."
8	Win 50 matches on one profile	The cover of the March 1996 issue of NBA Inside Stuff magazine.
9	Win 75 matches on one profile	The cover of the January 1996 issue of NBA Inside Stuff magazine.
10	Win 100 matches on one profile	The cover of the January 1998 issue of NBA Inside Stuff magazine.
11	Win 5 matches in a row	The cover of the June 2002 issue of NBA Inside Stuff magazine. In this issue Inside Stuff tells the story of Jerry Stackhouse and interviews Kevin Garnett.
12	Win 10 matches in a row	The cover of the May 1994 issue of Hoop magazine.
13	Win 15 matches in a row	1994 Preseason NBA Inside Stuff magazine cover shot.
14	Win 20 matches in a row	The cover of the May 2001 issue of NBA Inside Stuff magazine.
15	Win 25 matches in a row	The cover of the April 1999 issue of NBA Inside Stuff magazine. In this issue Inside Stuff goes behind the scene with Shaq, the players of the NBA tell you why their Mom is the greatest and Kobe speaks on Magic.
16	Beat Shaq with a point guard	The cover of the February 1998 Hoop magazine.
17	Beat Yao Ming with a point guard	The cover of the January 2001 issue of NBA Inside Stuff magazine. In this issue Inside Stuff takes a look at the ""New Blood"" rising in the NBA, Darius Miles and Lattrell Sprewell are interviewed and more.

#	Required to Unlock	Desription
18	Beat Tim Duncan w/o losing a round	The cover of the May 2002 issue of NBA Inside Stuff magazine. This issue includes a feature on why the 2002 Western Conference may be the strongest ever.
19	Beat Vince Carter at his house	The cover of the March 2001 issue of NBA Inside Stuff magazine.
20	Beat Jason Kidd with a created player	The cover of the April 1996 issue of NBA Inside Stuff magazine.
21	Beat Kobe Bryant at the Italian Villa	The cover of the December 2000 issue of NBA Inside Stuff magazine. IS guesses who the next super star is going to be, behind the scenes of what goes into making a hoops video game and Kidd and Hardaway speak on the best backcourt in the NBA.
22	Beat Chris Webber at the Italian Villa	The cover of the April 2002 issue of NBA Inside Stuff magazine.
23	Beat Steve Francis and give up 3 dunks or less	The cover of the December 1993 issue of NBA Inside Stuff magazine.
24	Beat Tracy McGrady at his house	The cover of the January 1997 issue of NBA Inside Stuff magazine.
25	Beat Kevin Garnett without losing a round	The cover of the April 1986 Hoop magazine.
26	Beat Dirk Nowitzki at the Malone residence	The cover of the November 1996 issue of NBA Inside Stuff magazine.
27	Beat Paul Pierce without giving up a turnover	The cover of the October 1999 issue of NBA Inside Stuff magazine. In this issue Inside Stuff takes an in-depth look at Tim Duncan, Damon Stoudemire speaks on Isiah Thomas and 24 questions with Darrell Armstrong.
28	Beat Antoine Walker without giving up a 3-pt shot	The cover of the December 1992 issue of Hoop magazine.
29	Beat Allen Iverson without giving up a steal	The cover of the December 1985 issue of Hoop magazine.
30	Beat Elton Brand by holding him to 12 points or less in the match	The cover of the Summer 1989 issue of Hoop magazine.
31	Beat Grant Hill by holding him to 10 points or less in the match	The cover of the May 1985 issue of Hoop magazine.
32	Beat Dr J with a created player	The cover of the March 1988 issue of Hoop magazine.
33	Mar, 1996 NBA Inside Stuff Magazine	Beat Wilt Chamberlain and block 3 shots in the process
34	Beat Larry Bird without losing a round	The cover of the Summer 1987 issue of Hoop magazine.

#	Required to Unlock	Desription
35	Beat Magic Johnson without committing a foul	The cover of the June 1986 issue of Hoop magazine.
36	Beat Julius Irving	The cover of the February 2001 issue of Hoop magazine.
37	Beat Bill Russell while holding him to less than FG% - 40%	The cover of the April 1988 Hoop Magazine.
38	Beat Dominique Wilkins without giving up a dunk	The cover of the December 1999 issue of Hoop magazine.
39	Beat Wilt Chamberlain while holding him to less than FG% - 30%	The cover of the May 1991 issue of Hoop magazine.
40	Beat Walt Frazier and give up less than two 3-pt shots	The cover of the November 1984 issue of Hoop magazine.
41	Win a round by not missing a shot	The cover of the May 1992 issue of Hoop magazine.
42	Win a match by not missing a shot	The cover of the February 2000 issue of Hoop magazine.
43	Win a round in 30 sec or less	The cover of the July 2001 issue of NBA Inside Stuff magazine.
44	Win a match in 30 sec or less	The cover of the April 2000 issue of NBA Inside Stuff magazine.
45	Win a match by holding your opponent to 0 points	The cover of the November 2000 issue of NBA Inside Stuff magazine.
46	Make 3 consecutive 2-pt shots in a round	The cover of an issue of Hoop magazine, featuring Steve Francis on the cover.
47	Make 7 consecutive 2-pt shots in a match	The cover of the September 2001 issue of NBA Inside Stuff magazine.
48	Make 10 consecutive 2-pt shots in a match	The cover of the June 1999 issue of NBA Inside Stuff magazine. Inside Stuff interviews superstar Vince Carter, the looks and style of the NBA players off-the-court are showcased and KG speaks on prepping for the Olympics.
49	Win a round by only shooting 2- pt shots	The cover of the November 1998 issue of Inside Stuff magazine.
50	Win a match by only shooting 2-pt shots	The cover of the March 1998 issue of NBA Inside Stuff magazine.
51	Win a round and shoot higher than 75% from 2-pt range	The cover of the March 1997 issue of NBA Inside Stuff magazine.
52	Win a match and shoot higher than 80% from 2-pt range	The cover of the January 1989 issue of Hoop magazine.
53	Make a 2-pt shot in the first 5 seconds of a round	The cover the December 1986 issue of Hoop magazine.
54	Win a match and make a 2-pt shot	The cover of the May 1994 issue of NBA Inside Stuff magazine.
55	Make a match winning 2-pt jump shot	The cover of the June 1995 issue of NBA Inside Stuff magazine.
56	Make a 3-pt shot in the first 5 seconds of a round	The cover of the November 2001 issue of NBA Inside Stuff magazine.
57	Make three 3-pt shots in a round	The cover of the June 1991 issue of Hoop magazine.
58	Make nine 3-pt shots in a match	The cover of the July 1997 issue of NBA Inside Stuff magazine.

#	Required to Unlock	Desription
59	Make two consecutive 3-pt shots	The cover of the September 1997 issue of NBA Inside Stuff magazine.
60	Win a round by only shooting 3-pt shots	The cover of the May 1987 issue of Hoop magazine.
61	Win a match by only shooting 3-pt shots	The cover of the September 1998 issue of NBA Inside Stuff magazine.
62	Win a match by shooting 80% or higher from 3-pt range	The cover of the April 1985 issue of Hoop magazine.
63	Make a 3-pt shot from either corner	The cover of the March 2001 issue of Hoop magazine.
64	Make a 3-pt shot from at least 3 feet behind the line	The cover of the October 2002 issue of NBA Inside Stuff magazine.
65	Make a match winning 3-pt shot	The cover of the November 1997 issue of NBA Inside Stuff magazine.
66	Make 2 free throws in one match	The cover of the October 1994 issue of NBA Inside Stuff magazine.
67	Grab an offensive rebound from your own missed free throw	The cover of the Summer 1986 issue of Hoop magazine.
68	Make a free throw off the backboard (bank shot)	The cover of the May 2003 issue of NBA Inside Stuff magazine.
69	Make 3 dunks in one round	The cover of the February 2000 issue of NBA Inside Stuff magazine.
70	Make 5 dunks in one round	The cover of the December 2002 issue of NBA Inside Stuff magazine. In this issue Carter's ""other-worldly serenity"" is revealed, news on Shareef Abdur-Rahim's return to Atlanta, and a 24 question interview with T-Mac.
71	Make 10 dunks in one match	Clyde the Glide Drexler graces the cover of the May 1987 issue of Hoop magazine.
72	Win a round by only using dunks	The cover of the January 2001 issue of Hoop Magazine.

FRIENDS

#	Friend	Required to Unlock
1	Teresa	Win a match by only using dunks
2	Anna	Make a dunk in the first five seconds of a round
3	Ricky	Make a round winning dunk
4	Blanca	Make a match winning dunk
5	Alexa	Dunk the ball (i.e. Posterize) over Shaq
6	Eli	Dunk the ball (i.e. Posterize) over Mutombo
7	Johanna	Grab 3 offensive rebounds in one round
8	Kristen	Grab 7 offensive rebounds in one match

FRIENDS

#	Friend	Required to Unlock
9	Trevor	Grab 10 offensive rebounds in one match
10	Tisha	Grab an offensive rebound off your own missed 3-pt shot
11	Mary	Grab an offensive rebound in the first 5 seconds of a round
12	Kazuki	Grab a rebound by diving for a loose ball
13	Amber	Grab 3 defensive rebounds in one round
14	Katrina	Grab 7 defensive rebounds in one match
15	Greg	Grab 12 defensive rebounds in one match
16	Susan	Grab a defensive rebound in the first 5 seconds of a round
17	Sharon	Block 3 shots in one round
18	Reggie B.	Block 5 shots in one round
19	Leslie	Block 10 shots in one match
20	Tamayra	Block 5 shots in one match
21	Johnny	Block 10 shots in one match
22	Lahonda	Block three 3-pt shots in one match
23	Vivica	Block a dunk
24	Reggie S.	Block a center's shot with a point guard

BIG SHOTS

#	Description	Required to Unlock
1	2001 NBA East All-Star Team	Block 3 Shaq shots in one match
2	Kobe, Shaq, & Magic after winning the 2002 NBA Finals	Block a shot in the first 5 seconds of a round
3	Ginobili on a breakaway dunk	Steal the ball 4 times in one round
4	2001 NBA West All-Star Team	Steal the ball 7 times in one match
5	Tony Parker at center court	Steal the ball 10 times in one match
6	Chris Webber up against Al Harrington	Steal the ball on 3 consecutive possessions
7	Iverson with 10 steals on May 13, 1999 against Orlando	Steal the ball in the first 5 seconds of a round
8	Dr J scoring 24 on the last game of his career	Successfully draw 3 charging fouls in one round
9	Celtics winning game 5 of the 1987 Finals	Successfully draw 6 charging fouls in one match
10	Dominique Wilkins flying high	Successfully draw a charge in the first 5 seconds of a round
11	Mutombo and the Nuggets upset Seattle in the 1st round of the '94 playoffs	Force the opponent into 3 turnovers in one round
12	Portland & Phoenix in the highest scoring NBA playoff game	Force the opponent into 10 turnovers in one match
13	Jamal Mashburn towering over Chris Childs	Win a round without committing a turnover

#	Description	Required to Unlock
14	Allan Houston from deep	Win a match without committing a turnover
15	John Paxson in game 4 of the 1993 Finals	Win a round without committing a foul
16	1997's #1 pick Tim Duncan	Win a match without committing a foul
17	Scottie Pippen & Jeff Hornacek at the United Center in Chicago	Win a match by committing 3 fouls or less
18	Isiah Thomas scoring 43 in a game 6 loss to the Lakers in the '89 Finals	Win a match in spite of committing a minimum of 10 fouls
19	Steve Nash spots up over Mike Bibby	Beat Nate Archibald
20	San Francisco's Rick Barry scores 57 against the Knicks on Dec 14, 1965	Beat Tim Duncan
21	Moses Malone grabs 10 offensive boards in one quarter in 1992	Beat Robert Parish
22	John Stockton hits the game winning jumper in Game six of the '97 Western Semifinals	Beat Larry Bird
23	Bill Walton in San Diego, 1980	Beat Kevin McHale
24	Yao Ming lets a hook shot go over Shaq	Beat Isiah Thomas
25	Drexler brings the crowd to its feet in 1996	Beat Walt Frazier
26	Pippen commits 12 turnovers against Houston on Jan 30, 1996	Beat Darryl Dawkins
27	The Celtics go 50-1 at Boston Garden in the 1985-86 season	Win a match by holding your opponent to 0 offensive rebounds
28	Stockton dishes out 24 assists vs. the Lakers in game 5 of the '88 semifinals	Win a match by holding your opponent to 0 dunks
29	Stockton becomes the all-time consecutive game assist leader	Win a match by holding your opponent to 0 3-pt shots
30	Game three of the 1995 Finals between Houston and Orlando	Win a match by holding your opponent to 0 steals
31	Robert Parish counts his 20,000th point on Jan 17, 1992	Win a match by holding your opponent to 0 blocks
32	The Celtics Dynasty	Win a match and don't let them get on fire.
33	Darryl Dawkins of Philly records eight blocks in a playoff game vs. Atlanta	Beat Bill Walton
34	Jason Kidd & Gary Payton in game 6 of the 2003 Eastern Conference Playoffs	Win a round by holding your opponent to 3 points or less
35	Duncan, MVP of the 1999 NBA Finals	Win a round by holding your opponent to 0 points
36	Kenyon Martin challenging Tim Duncan with a drive to the hoop in the 2003 Finals	Win a match by holding your opponent to 2 points
37	James Worthy records his only triple-double in game 7 of the '88 Finals	Win a match without losing a round
38	Magic hands out 21 assists in game 3 of the '84 Finals	Win a match by holding your opponent to 8 points or less

#	Description	Required to Unlock
39	Wilt Chamberlain knocks down 73 point against Chicago, 1962	Beat Oscar Robertson
40	Kobe Bryant dazzling the crowd in the 2002 Finals against the Nets	Beat Rick Barry
41	Shaq on the Lakers jet after sweeping the Nets in the 2002 Finals	Beat James Worthy
42	Shaq attempts a record 39 free throws in a 2000 finals game vs. Indiana	Beat Kareem Abdul-Jabbar
43	Scottie Pippen raises the Championship trophy after game six of the '96 finals	Beat Magic Johnson
44	Stephon Marbury takes it to the hole against Tony Parker and the Spurs	Beat Wilt Chamberlain
45	Yao Ming and the Rockets battle Ben Wallace and the Pistons	Beat Earl Monroe
46	Karl Malone becomes the first player to reach 2,000 points in 10 consecutive seasons	Beat Willis Reed
47	Magic Johnson becomes the 1991 All-Star game MVP	Beat Moses Malone
48	Robert Parish becomes the all-time leader for most NBA seasons played	Beat Clyde Drexler

MIDWAY EXTRAS

#	Description	Required to Unlock
1	An early "moodboard" of an interface featuring T-Mac and KG	Beat George Gervin
2	A pre-production sketch of the NBA Ballers design	Beat Wes Unseld
3	VC & KG during an All-Star game shoot	Beat Elton Brand
4	A robot hoop and backboard concept that was cut from the game	Beat Kobe Bryant without losing a round
5	Details on the robot's transformation.	Beat Shaq without losing a round
6	A caricature of John Vignocchi, an NBA Ballers designer	Beat Allen Iverson without losing a round
7	A character study of Jason Williams during pre-production	Beat Kobe Bryant with a created player
8	A "super-human" sketch of Vince Carter	Beat Allen Iverson with a created player
9	A painting of Allen Iverson	Beat Mike Bibby with a created player
10	A sketch of Chris Webber for use	Beat Yao Ming with a created player
11	One of over 100 concepts for an in-game screen	Beat Steve Francis with a created player
12	A "still life" photo of Stephon Marbury and some locker room "bling"	Beat Kevin Garnett with a created player
13	A concept sketch of a farm court in Indiana	Beat Ben Wallace with a created player
14	An early sketch of a pensive "Stevie Franchise"	Beat LeBron James with a created player
15	Another sketch of the transforming robot, M.A.G.N.U.M.	Win 5 collectible images in one match

#	Description	Required to Unlock
16	A glimpse into the baller life	Win 100,000 credits in "your jackpot"
17	T-Mac and Grant Hill all dressed up	Play a match at a Rags 2 Riches create-a-mansion
18	The Midway Sports Mascot	Play a match against Kobe Bryant at a create-a-mansion
19	A Ballers logo that didn't quite make the cut	Play a match against Shaq at a create-a-mansion
20	Marbury posing for the camera	Play a match against LeBron James at a create-a-mansion
21	Marbury showing off his handles in his own driveway	Play a match against Magic Johnson at a create-a-mansion
22	Another concept for the Ballers art Style	Earn 500,000 credits on a user profile
23	Shaq Diesel relaxing in his rec room at his L.A. crib	Earn 1,000,000 credits on a user profile
24	A schematic of the NBA Ballers animation system	Earn 3,000,000 credits on a user profile
25	A Tokyo street court that didn't make the final cut	Earn 5,000,000 credits on a user profile

BALLER'S CINEMA

Wait-there's more! Sit down with a bag of popcorn and open up Baller's Cinema. Certain clips will need to be unlocked through gameplay.

OPENING MOVIE

Miss it the first time? Check out the NBA Ballers opening movie.

FILM VAULT

The following movies will unlock at certain points in the game. Check back often to see what has become available.

FILM VAULT CLIPS

FILE #	FILM TITLE	FILE #	FILM TITLE
1	ANTONIO DAVIS	27	MAGIC JOHNSON
2	ANTAWN JAMISON	28	MICHAEL FINLEY 1
3	BEN WALLACE	29	MICHAEL FINLEY 2
4	BIG NICKNAMES	30	MIKE BIBBY
5	CHRIS WEBBER	31	NBA HAIRCUTS
6	DARRYL DAWKINS	32	NICKNAMES
7	DIRK NOWITZKI	33	PAU GASOL
8	DOMINIQUE WILKINS	34	PAUL PIERCE 1
9	EDDIE JONES	35	PAUL PIERCE 2
10	ELTON BRAND	36	PETE MARAVICH
11	FRANCIS AND MOBLEY	37	RASHARD LEWIS
12	GARY PAYTON 1	38	RAY ALLEN
13	GARY PAYTON 2	39	REGGIE MILLER
14	GARY PAYTON 3	40	SHAQ MOTION CAPTURE
15	JERRY STACKHOUSE 1	41	SHAQ NICKNAMES
16	HOW TO STOP THE LAKERS	42	SHAQ THE STRONGEST MAN
17	JALEN ROSE	43	SHAREEF ABDHUR-RAHIM
18	JASON KIDD	44	STEPHON MARBURY
19	JASON TERRY	45	STEVE FRANCIS 1
20	JERMAINE O'NEAL 1	46	STEVE FRANCIS 2
21	JERMAINE O'NEAL 2	47	TRACY MCGRADY
22	JERRY STACKHOUSE 2	48	VINCE CARTER 1
23	KARL MALONE	49	VINCE CARTER 2
24	KEITH VAN HORN	50	WALLY SZCZERBIAK 1
25	KEVIN GARNETT	51	WALLY SZCZERBIAK 2
26	KOBE BRYANT	52	WALT FRAZIER

CREDITS

Want to pay the publishers and developers the proper respect? Browse through the credits to see the people behind the game.

DVD EXTRAS

Check out an exclusive Behind the Ballers video and a special Stephon Marbury animated, ball-handling promo clip in the DVD Extras menu.

TOURNAMENT CODES

The following three button code combinations will unlock many different types of gameplay modes. Match these codes with the proper logo combinations on the load screen before a match.

PYGMY...................................... 425

RANDOM MOVES 300

TOURNAMENT MODE 011

BIG HEAD 134

BABY BALLERS (BOTH PLAYERS MUST AGREE)....... 423

PAPER BALLERS (BOTH PLAYERS MUST AGREE) 354

KID BALLERS (BOTH PLAYERS MUST AGREE) 433

YOUNG BALLERS (BOTH PLAYERS MUST AGREE) ...443

SHOW SHOT % 012

ALTERNATE GEAR 123

FIRE ABILITY ENABLED 722

EXPANDED MOVES SET 512

SUPER BLOCKS 124

SUPER PUSH 315

GREAT HANDLES

PLAY AS COACH

PLAY AS AGENT

PLAY AS SECRETARY 547

PLAY AS BUSINESS MAN ONE 537

PLAY AS BUSINESS MAN TWO 527

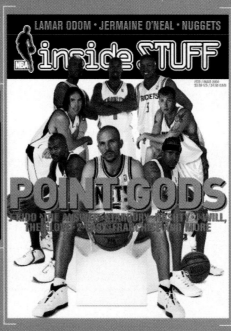
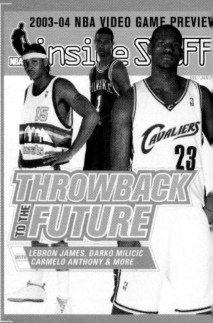

GO BEHIND THE SCENES LIKE NEVER BEFORE

AUTHORIZED PERSONNEL ONLY

NBA

Go right to the Source! NBA TV – your All-Access Pass for everything Basketball. Don't miss Live Games in amazing Hi-Definition, Exclusive Playoff action and original programs – NBA TV Insiders, Real Training Camp, the Entertainers Basketball Classic at Rucker Park and more!

Contact your local cable or satellite provider today!

It's Fan-tastic!